"Joe Costello's ambitic
down with this book a
it go? Costello offers sc
cover this tarnished bi........... ....
is an audacious proposition, argued confidently by a true small-d
democrat." —William Greider, Author of *Come Home, America: The
Rise and Fall (and Redeeming Promise) of Our Country*

"Joe Costello is a lifelong student of democracy, the millenia-old,
still radical idea of self-government. His deeply original diagnosis
of our contemporary woes bears careful scrutiny for its shredding
of the illusions that prop up both right and left. It's impossible to
think about banking, finance, energy, technology, or politics the
same way after reading *Of, By, For*, so do not delay." —Mitch Kapor,
Partner, Kapor Capital.

"Everyone lucky enough to have a conversation with Joe Costello
has walked away fizzing with ideas and possibilities. In these
pages, the intellectual thrills are yours for the taking. You'll find a
personal economics tutorial, history lesson, and civics anthem
from a mind as comfortable with Heraclitus as with Blade Runner
and OPEC. Joe's first book is the coming-out party of an important
public intellectual." —Raj Patel, author of *The Value of Nothing*

"Check your ideology at the door. If you feel our economics and
politics are broken, Joe Costello not only explains the ruinous cor-
rosion of both but why, we, as citizens must rethink and rebuild
the future on a much more sane foundation." —Joe Trippi, author
of *The Revolution Will Not Be Televised*

"America has lost its way. An empire-driven culture of greed and lies has come close to wrecking the republic. Joe Costello sees what has happened with a clarity that will disturb you, but he also sees a way forward that can give you some optimism—if you're willing to do something about it. His prescription starts with the simple idea that we cannot begin to fix what is broken solely by targeting politicians at the top of the pyramid; the soul of democracy, which is more about participating than simply voting, is in our local communities and neighborhoods." —Dan Gillmor, author of *We the Media: Grassroots Journalism by the People, for the People* and *Mediactive*

"This red hot shrapnel of an e book is all about liberation—the liberation of our country from a bloated financial sector which neither political party intends to take on. Joe Costello is as scathing as Tom Paine, or William Lloyd Garrison, and he is as determined as they were to expose the particular form that oppression takes today. Like them he is making a case for more democracy. Read it and pass it on, so that in our time Joe Costello gets the kind of hearing that Paine and Garrison received in theirs." —Thomas Geoghegan, Lawyer and author of *Were You Born on the Wrong Continent?*

"Vaclav Havel said that the success of the Velvet Revolution in Czechoslovakia had actually been shaped years before by a brave handful of individuals who were willing to 'live in truth' and not succumb to the absurdity of the prevailing political order. This is a perfect description of Joe Costello's often lonely quest to speak truth about America and its failed political class without favor to political partisanship or false ideology. *Of, By, For* is a fervent affirmation of the imperative for a renaissance of American Democracy and a roadmap to get there." —Patrick Caddell

OF BY FOR

THE NEW POLITICS OF
MONEY, DEBT & DEMOCRACY

BY JOSEPH COSTELLO

For Jim and Mary Costello

I am part of all that I have met

Jim
we need to
revive and
evolve our
Democracy all of us.

John

6/9/12

TABLE OF CONTENTS

INTRODUCTION

Of, By, For is a compilation of thoughts, analysis, and short essays on American politics. The underlying theme; American politics is both corrupt and dysfunctional. Its conclusion; American political economy must be democratically reformed, using both the knowledge we have from the past and imagination for the future.

Although this is a work about American politics, you will not find reference to the present election campaigns or candidates, nor little about liberal or conservative, and Democrat or Republicans. Any mention of the two latter categories inevitably deals with their culpability and complicity in our increasingly destructive political dysfunction.

The book acknowledges and places in context the historical uniqueness of the American Republic, noting as historian Gore Vidal has said, across recorded Western history, self-government is an anomaly. It is this historical uniqueness that should be highly treasured.

I seek to help define, redefine, and most importantly expand the components of what presently is popularly considered politics. I look seriously at banking, finance, debt, the corporation, technology, our physical environment, and money, describing how these are all political entities, seriously lacking in democratic structure and process.

The entire work advocates democracy as the cure for our political ills. I offer a historical perspective on the processes and structures of self-government, hopefully offering ideas on how we can reform and evolve democracy for the 21st century. This is done with the understanding, that democracy, at its foundation, needs an educated, active, and trusted citizenry.

Finally, this book is not structured as a traditional narrative. While each chapter is cohesive, I also invite dipping and skipping around to subsections, which I believe each offer a thought, a catalyst for thinking. This book is a call for the American people to reclaim their rights and responsibilities. Most importantly, it is a call for participation in this great democratic experiment, to not do so, would be both a rejection of our heritage and a condemnation of the future.

Joe Costello
5/16/2012

I. REFORMING DEMOCRACY

1. CATALYZING REFORM

We don't need a revolution in America, we need a reformation. Our political economy has become top heavy and eminently corrupt. Our economy is controlled by and for a few gigantic corporations. Our politics run by a small, unrepresentative, professional political class, who do the bidding of these corporations. Technology has massively changed our politics and most have voluntarily disengaged from being citizens. We are fed a vapid fear-laden death cult of patriotism, instead of building a life-affirming culture of courage and the necessary work to being a citizen. Yet, as long as it flows somewhere in us, the fount of democracy is eternal and renewal possible.

The answer to political despair is to engage political life. Anger is many times the first step, yet it needs to be accompanied by wisdom, an appreciation of wondrous life. The answer to political despair is not political faith, but political life. In response to the poli-tics of despair and our Xanax peddlers, try Roy Batty's answer in *Blade Runner*, "More life, fucker."

* * *

"The idea at the heart of the Polish movement—and indeed, all serious democratic movements—was that broad sectors of peo-ple without power could join together to have a genuine say about those things that affect them the most. It is an immensely appealing idea but an embattled one, because people do not gen-erally believe its goal is possible beyond very narrow limits and therefore, are afraid to run the risks necessary to achieve it. It is not simply "fear" or "apathy" that immobilizes people; it is knowledge they have been taught about how power works in their lives, in their jobs, in their neighborhoods, and, indeed, in most of their social relations. They desire change, yet do not be-lieve they can get much of it." —Lawrence Goodwyn, *Breaking the Barrier*

In Lawrence Goodwyn's *Breaking the Barrier*, an important his-tory of the Polish reform movement Solidarity, he examines the evolution of a reform movement and its necessary components. One important step for any reform movement is to create a space outside of the established system, allowing for discussion, organi-zation, and then action outside what is officially sanctioned or ac-cepted. In Goodwyn's history, this space was created first in the kitchens of Poland, reaching a critical mass or maybe appropriately a "critical space" in the shipyards of Gdansk. Goodwyn writes,

"The deeper reality was that the entire postwar effort of Polish workers to break out of party control on the shop floor can be properly understood as an organizational attempt to escape party censorship. Additionally, of course, the very existence of massively organized social space independent of the party carried profound ramifications for the Leninist system of governance. Solidarnosc was "political" from its very inception."

Of course while our present political system is not, at this point, as oppressive as communist Poland, it does have rigorously defined and controlled meanings for acceptable politics, a very entrenched political class, and a corporate political media, working very diligently to confine political debate. The average person has no contact with politics outside of these established channels, if they even have that. Their role in established politics is limited to voting and for a very insignificant few, giving some money and time to a campaign every few years. This has created a citizenry distressingly disenfranchised, whose mobilization into an active force for reform faces different, but just as real barriers, as the Poles of the 1980s.

We need to get beyond the Democratic/Republican, Liberal/Conservative definitions strangling our politics, and begin to create a reform politics transcending an increasingly corrupted electoral system, though it will at some point have to interact in this system. A space is needed that opens political possibilities beyond those found in the pages of *The New York Times*, babbled by the political class, and by those clinging to an insolvent left/right divide.

This is an extremely difficult endeavor because the small minority of people who follow and engage in politics bring with them all the baggage of their present political identities. While the vast majority desire change, as Goodwyn states, they "do not believe they can get much of it." There are two barriers to cross; getting the few with political identities to move beyond them, and more importantly, to engage the vast majority, who logically see no ability to effect change.

Reform of our political economy will not come through established channels. If we want reform, the first thing to create is reform space.

* * *

"SNCC (Student Nonviolent Coordinating Committee) activities within the broader (civil rights) movement reshaped the republican tradition as it was widely understood in American life. From the colonial period forward, this tradition had depended on the vision of independent yeoman—each with a stake in society—gathering to stand against distant, impersonal, and overbearing institutions. SNCC revised this republican idea of standing up to demand one's natural rights to life, liberty, and property. The struggle to realize democratic social relations was an avenue of public work that was possible only in the company of others. SNCC workers demonstrated the simple proposition that one cannot live a democratic life alone." —Wesley C. Hogan, *Many Minds, One Heart*

A few years ago, I visited Atlanta. My first stop was the Martin Luther King memorial in the heart of the city. I have to admit that, the memorial and its buildings were not only underwhelming, but they seemed to lack the memory of life. The whole thing was very cold and sterile until I walked to the one corner of the complex where the old red-bricked Ebenezer church stands.

Walking into the church, the past instantly comes to life. A half century before, in this and hundreds of others even smaller churches, in small community rooms, and living rooms spread across the South, one of the great democratic movements in American history was birthed and organized. Standing in the small church, one seems instantly connected to and overwhelmed by the astounding accomplishments of the former slave population of this republic, who standing together, nonviolently gained the citizen enfranchisement denied them for a century after emancipation.

This memory was revived as I read Wesley Hogan's *Many Minds, One Heart*, an excellent work on American history concerning the founding and actions of the Student Nonviolent Coordinating Committee (SNCC). SNCC was an important element of the Civil Rights Movement. Across the South, students helped inspire and de-centrally organize direct action campaigns against segregation and for political enfranchisement. Hogan's book is essential history, written with a small "d" democratic knowledge and understanding sorely lacking from far too much American history.

For us today, *Many Minds, One Heart* is extremely valuable. It unfolds a story of the thinking and actions of the disenfranchised coming together to demand their natural rights as human beings and their political rights as citizens. "Gathering," Hogan writes, "to stand against distant, impersonal, and overbearing institutions." This is the challenge we Americans face today. Both voluntarily and through subtle coercion, the majority of Americans have become disenfranchised from any meaningful politics. It is time for us to "gather against distant, impersonal, and overbearing institutions."

Just as SNCC helped to define and enfranchise a disenfranchised people, so must we. Our republic needs to redefine what it means to be a citizen in the 21st century. We need to rebuild and evolve new practices by which citizens discuss, interact, and implement politics. We need to develop a citizen culture, and most importantly as a society, value the hard work of being a citizen.

SNCC overcame two great barriers. The first was fear. Today, America is an extremely fearful, bordering on paranoid society. Much of this flows from our disenfranchisement, from our feelings of powerlessness. SNCC met this fear by bringing people together in small groups to discuss the challenges they faced, showing people they were not alone. Despite overwhelming odds, people had the space to act, persevere, and triumph. One of the Freedom Riders explained simply, "I lost my fear."

The second barrier SNCC confronted was the wide held belief of political impotence, the decadent belief that one person's actions had neither impact nor value. In the apartheid South, whites were politically enfranchised. Every single day the black community saw and experienced oppressive political power. Today, while people are not legally disenfranchised, they are effectively impotent when it comes to their politics.

One SNCC member explained, "I once thought politics was what you were for or against—not what you did." This is a key understanding for changing our present situation. In breaking the barriers of disenfranchisement and fear, we need to bring people together to redefine politics and create a politics not of "for or against," but a politics of doing. The first and most crucial step, as SNCC understood, is simply to bring people together in small meetings—Ebenezer churches, libraries, living rooms—and begin democratic conversations. We must discuss the issues of our time and how they impact each person in their daily lives. Without the initiation of these small conversations, there can be no political revival. Two things need to come out of these conversations, one is a necessary new political dialogue and the other is a will to do.

In these conversations, we must reintroduce a very important aspect missing from our politics—democratic patience. Hogan does an excellent job in describing this most important aspect of democratic culture. Democratic patience was not about waiting ten more years for Jim Crow to end, another five for the vote, or in our time for the end of Wall Street dominance of the economy. Democratic patience is the ability to talk about difficult problems with each other, especially with those whom we disagree. We can start by developing patience with those who we agree with, and then begin to engage those with whom we disagree.

Today, democratic patience is absent from all aspects of our politics. The idiocy calling itself political debate in this country is toxic. Our political class prizes zingers, not understanding and entertainment, not enlightenment. Without a healthy political dialogue, there can be no healthy politics, and without patience there can be no dialogue.

Out of democratic conversation must come democratic action. Once people are engaged they must have something to do. For SNCC it was desegregating diners, buses, and registering to vote. A big question is what constitutes democratic action today? I'll suggest two things; involvement in local government, and energy conservation. We can engage in local government in order to begin making necessary changes in our communities. We can begin a process of taking power away from Washington DC and the state capitals. This is the only way to begin fixing the corruption—drain the swamps. Energy conservation provides an opportunity for people to become actively involved at home, work, school, and in their community in order to kick America's destructive oil addiction.

From democratic conversations and democratic action will come democratic experience. As historian Lawrence Goodwyn has written, democracy is experiential—it is about learning and doing, the cornerstone of experience. As Hogan documents, SNCC was one big experiment and learning experience. She writes,

> "By pushing the boundaries, movement participants could see more clearly what was at stake...people saw a small number of individuals taking action and were inspired to join them; through the experiences they then shared, the activists and their recruits developed an understanding of what was possible—one that differed considerably from that of most blacks and whites in Mississippi."

SNCC was a group of disenfranchised people learning how to gain their political will, rights, and responsibilities. This is what is necessary for all of us to do today. Our contemporary politics knows little about democracy, yet we can begin to create, talk, act, learn, and learn some more. The most glaring problem with our present politics is it learns nothing, revealing one thing, our politics is not democratic, in fact it is oppressively doctrinaire.

Democratic conversations, patience, action and learning were foundational values and practices of SNCC. But the most encompassing value and practice of SNCC was nonviolence. Democracy is nonviolent, yet, a nagging question remains whether there can be a secular based nonviolence? I believe the answer to that is yes, and more importantly, our technological evolution makes it imperative for human survival.

Many Minds, One Heart should be widely read. I pulled from Hogan's book a couple of points that will help us revive our politics. Most important, the one basic fact of democratic evolution across history is that it moves up from the bottom. We must come together to reclaim, revive and evolve our politics. We must become citizens, and in so doing, we will gain meaning for ourselves. As one SNCC participant stated, "I had never had that much dignity before. It was exhilarating, it was something I had earned—the sense of independence that comes to a free person."

2. A DEMOCRATIC ETHOS

"*From a possible future.* — Is a state of affairs unthinkable in which the malefactor calls himself to account and publicly dictates his own punishment, in the proud feeling that he is thus honoring the law which he himself has made, that by punishing himself he is exercising his power, the power of the lawgiver? He may once offend, but by his voluntary punishment, he raises himself above his offense; he not only wipes out his offense by candor, greatness and calmness, but he adds to it a public benefit." —*Daybreak: Thoughts on the Prejudices of Morality*, Friedrich Wilhelm Nietzsche

Could there be a more antithetical ethos to our Wall Street "Masters of the Universe" or to our political class? In this tragic era of comic *ubermensch*, such a possible future seems further off than a century ago. Completely in opposition to his popular image, Nietzsche is one of the important and necessary democratic thinkers of history. I was reminded of this while reading the New York Times review of a new Nietzsche biography written by another infamous modern *ubermensch*, Francis Fukuyama. He is an eminent anti-democratic figure who came to the American intellectual fore-front with his book *The End of History*, which in no sense was meant to be ironic, making it simply ridiculous. He's a prominent figure of the reactionary school of "neo-conservatives" who reaped upon this republic untold damage. He is a propagator of anti-democratic screed, couched as ideas of "liberal democracy." None of this has kept him from holding a prestigious chair at John Hopkins University, the center of the American foreign policy establishment, nor has it kept his columns from regularly appearing in *The New York Times*. He deems himself some sort of philosopher.

Nietzsche was an anti-metaphysician, and, as he claimed, he philosophized with a hammer, which is funny. Nietzsche is very funny and if you read him and you're not laughing, you're missing the plot. As an anti-metaphysician, the good metaphysicians, if there is such a thing, dismiss him. They rightly point out that he has nothing to offer them. The bad philosophers, of which the 20th century is littered, pull out little tidbits, then attempt to build upon them elaborate scandalous schools of thought. Upon reading most of them you know why Nietzsche declared he wanted no disciples.

Mr. Fukuyama, as all bad metaphysicians, immediately grabs the easiest misinterpretation of Nietzsche—his concept of the "eternal re-occurrence." There was nothing metaphysical about this. It was an idea for life. In fact, it was completely anti-metaphysics. It is the idea that each of us should live as though we had only one life, which would be repeated exactly as lived, endlessly. It is difficult to come to conclusions about Nietzsche's thinking as a whole. He himself said he was busting down in order to rebuild, but he never got to that point before he collapsed. Of course, this doesn't stop Fukuyama from taking the great popular generalizations on Nietzsche's thinking and throwing them forward and twisting them for his purpose. Further down the piece, Mr. Fukuyama really lets loose in a way that exemplifies the tremendous intellectual dishonesty at the top of so much of our society, and what can only be described as the debauched thinking at the heart of neo-conservatism. He writes:

"Nietzsche, however, hoped for a future hierarchical society in which the labor of the many would support the greatness of the few, one in which the cultural cacophony of contemporary liberal societies would be replaced by the solidarity of a single, common culture...But understanding Nietzsche's project as a cultural rather than a political one should not blind us to its terrible implications. For while one might be able to create a small-scale community based on common and voluntary commitment to art, as Wagner sought to do in Bayreuth, scaling up such a project to society as a whole, with all its de facto diversity, would require dictatorial political power. The mystical origins of Nietzsche's Dionysian community are an open invitation to the unleashing of irrational passion that is perfectly happy to squander the life of any individual standing in its way. Ayatollah Khamenei is indeed a much better model of Nietzsche's future leader than the powerless Dalai Lama."

This is a purposeful misunderstanding of Nietzsche's thought, even more so of any democratic society. Can you imagine America's great poet of democracy, Walt Whitman, claiming that diversity required dictatorship, so too, the leaves of grass? At the bottom of Nietzsche's thought is the very democratic understanding of the necessity of the independent individual. It is the great paradox of democracy, independent individuals creating a collective social whole. Nietzsche spent much effort revealing the empowerment of the individual is in many ways antithetical to much of the canon of Western thought and morality, which is in many ways an ethos of subservience. Nietzsche tore at the fetters on the individual, asking how would you rebuild society if you were to place the independent individual at its foundation and then re-

build. Is that not democracy? Now, Nietzsche certainly was roman-
tic and took great poetic license. There's little argument he had a
taste for the myths of history's great men. But his tearing down
and looking to rebuild society based on life and the empowered individual is exactly what we must do if we are to evolve democracy.

Does Mr. Fukuyama understand this, or is he just another simple reactionary to Nietzsche's hammer? It is difficult to tell. The
neocons on the whole are an extremely intellectually dishonest
bunch, who like to throw around the words and symbols of our de-
cayed republic in an active effort to even more greatly undermine
it. He accuses Nietzsche of embracing "hierarchical" society, yet
the "liberal democracy," our corporatocracy that Mr. Fukuyama
previously labeled "the end of history," is as hierarchically structured a political economy as history has seen. Fukuyama's final in-
sult is to write,

> "Postmodernism, deconstructionism, cultural relativism, the
> "free spirit" scorning bourgeois morality, even New Age festi-
> vals like Burning Man can all ultimately be traced to him."

This is as low a blow as you can level at Nietzsche, the great
posthumous critic of the 20th century.

In his final years, Nietzsche began work on a series of books he
described as a "revaluation of values"—an attempt to rebuild what
the hammer had destroyed. He didn't come close to finishing it.
But others took it up, and instead of the effete rabble listed above
by Mr. Fukuyama, one of the most notably successful was Martin
Luther King Jr. Dr. King is the antithesis of the neo-conservatives'
intellectual dishonesty, militarism, and anti-life authoritarianism.
In his 1967 speech against the Vietnam War, Dr. King calls for a
"revolution of values" stating:

> "I am convinced that if we are to get on the right side of the
> world revolution, we as a nation must undergo a radical revolu-

tion of values. We must rapidly begin the shift from a thing-oriented society to a person-oriented society. When machines and computers, profit motives and property rights, are considered more important than people, the giant triplets of racism, extreme materialism, and militarism are incapable of being conquered."

Nietzsche never said it better.

* * *

When reading Thomas Jefferson, you become struck by Jefferson's animate advocacy of elections, elections for every organization. Elections, Jefferson correctly thought, were one of the keys to establishing democracy in an undemocratic world. Fast forward two centuries, and it's amazing how we take for granted what was once considered very, very radical. Some of those old dead white men were great advocates of equality and democracy at the same time that they were slaveholders. It's not just that we take our elections for granted, it is that we allow them to be co-opted and corrupted to the point where they are wreaking havoc over our system of self-government.

There are many factors contributing to the problems in our election processes, but none more so than the adoption of the tactics of marketing. Make no mistake, marketing is not politics. A pretty face, a seductive slogan, and a poster by the latest pop-artist are marketing mechanisms, not politics. Marketing is about selling products, it is about manipulation, and it has definite end. Politics is a process of education and deliberation and it is unending, continuous. The methods of polling, 30-second ads, and waves of big money destroyed the political institutions and processes necessary for a healthy self-government.

In any healthy democracy, the elections are only a necessary part of the political infrastructure. Today, they are the both the entire ends and means. Marketing and PR have replaced education and deliberation. Fifty years ago the preeminent thinker on technology's impact upon society, Marshall McLuhan, put it best,

> "Where advertising is heading is quite simply into a world where the ad will become a substitute for the product, and all the satisfactions will be derived informationally from the ad, and the product will be merely a number in some file somewhere."

What could better describe our supposed elected representatives in Washington DC: "merely numbers in a file somewhere."

* * *

> "You can't look around the world and not realize that we can be, and often are, extremely brutal and aggressive. And equally, we have inherited tendencies of love, compassion, and altruism, because they're there in the chimp. So, we've brought those with us. So, it's like each one of us has this dark side and a more noble side. And I guess it's up to each one of us to push one down and develop the other." —Jane Goodall

The entanglement of violence and civilization is as old as history, and as Goodall insightfully posits, prehistorical. Civilization is the antithesis of violence. Civilization is the means of human interaction beyond the physical intimidation of the fist, sword or gun. Nevertheless, violence remains a cornerstone of every civilization across history. Conjuring civilization from its violent underpinnings remains one of history's greatest acts of revolution. The 20th century was unprecedented in recorded history for bringing forth thought and action on recognizing and extracting violence from civilization's content.

Nonviolence is a political construct, comprised of millions of individuals, but four 20th century figures represent and helped define this civilizing movement, providing us with the glimpse of a path for the 21st century. These figures are Mohandas Gandhi in India, Martin Luther King Jr. in the United States, Mikhail Gorbachev in Russia, and Nelson Mandela in South Africa. Literally representing the four corners of the globe, these figures revealed the underlying violence of their respective cultures in an attempt to civilize anew. All would come to conclude, in the words of Dr. King, that what the world needed was a "revolution of values."

We can begin with Gandhi, who became a great figure in the politics of nonviolence by helping lead the Indian independence movement from Britain. Gandhi began his politics in South Africa at the turn of the 19th and 20th centuries. South Africa, as India, was under the rule of the British Empire. Asians in South Africa were second-class citizens, as were the native Africans. Using nonviolent tactics, Gandhi helped organize against some of the most egregiously racist of British laws. He would return to India and for four decades fight for Indian independence. The great lesson of Gandhi was that all oppression held a component of violence. Time and custom blended this violence into the background. The key element of engaged political nonviolence is to bring the violence of the system to the forefront, no longer bowing to it. This is done by no longer following established custom. Citizens take a public blow to reveal the system's underlying violence. Gandhi was a sublime character and maybe no more so than for his faith in humanity. Anyone who could publicly say they were relying on the underlying humanity of the English, despite all proven evidence to the contrary, was quite extraordinary.

Martin Luther King Jr. would take Gandhi's practices and thought and help turn them into one of the most powerful democratic forces in American history. The Civil Rights Movement saw a population, only two and three generations removed from the

shackles of slavery, revitalize and redefine the words and principles of one of history's few republics. The American republic—the
fount for defining much of what came to be known as self-government in the modern era—was two centuries before birthed with the
violent and abhorrent institution of slavery. A century later, the
abolition of slavery was accompanied with the rise of state-sanc-
tioned segregation, politically and economically disenfranchising
the majority of America's black population for almost another century.

The nights in jail, beatings, the dogs of Bull Conner, and mur-
ders were all in response to the black population actively rejecting
Jim Crow, publicly revealing the violence at the system's foundation. Despite all proven evidence to the contrary, MLK had faith in
white America. In the last year of his life, Dr. King developed a
"Poor People's" campaign, a beginning to the rejection of the violence of poverty. Violence remains the great invisible hand beneath
much of our economics. It needs to be brought to the surface if we
are to civilize our economy.

The third figure is Mikhail Gorbachev. Unlike Mr. Gandhi and
Mr. King, Gorbachev never claimed adherence to nonviolence, yet
he undertook one of the greatest and most unprecedented acts of
nonviolence in human history. He allowed the peaceful disintegra-
tion of the Soviet Union. When calls for independence in Eastern
Europe gained steam in the late 80s, they were not met with violence from Moscow. When the Berlin Wall collapsed and Mr. Gorbachev had a half-million troops in East Germany, they remained
in their barracks. Despite all proven evidence to the contrary, Mr.
Gorbachev had a great faith in humanity. This lesson remains particularly relevant for today's United States.

Finally, there is Nelson Mandela. Mr. Mandela is another who
never professed nonviolence. The ANC, of which he was a member, fought a very bloody war for decades across southern Africa.
For most of that time Mr. Mandela was imprisoned, this time he re-

garded as "wasted life." In the early 90s, as the apartheid regime came to its last days, the government sent Mr. Mandela a letter asking him to renounce violence and they would release him. Mr. Mandela responded wryly, saying his present position under the forceful hands of the state allowed him to take no such free position.

It was upon his release and his ascendancy to the South African presidency where Mr. Mandela would add a new chapter to the lessons of nonviolence. He was both forgiving and non-vindictive, incredibly so. Nothing can be so violent and brutal as righteous vengeance, and the vast majority of South Africans certainly had righteous justice on their side. Despite all proven evidence to the contrary, Nelson Mandela had faith in white South Africa. The power of forgiveness might be the most extraordinary of political weapons, yet forgiveness cannot begin until power is held accountable, an unjust system overturned, and the violence of power upended.

* * *

"Lo, you trust in the staff of this broken reed; on which if a man lean, it will go into his hand, and pierce it." —Isaiah 36:6

We see the development of a "new" politics, where a small group, known as technocrats, governs. This group, considered beyond politics, is comprised of purveyors of fundamental knowledge and wisdom transcending politics—so we are told. Simultaneously, the nullity at the foundation of Western politics becomes ever clearer to all. The disenfranchisement of the vast majority is distressingly vivid. Seemingly their only political act is public protest, confirming both their own weakness and the ineptitude of the governing cabal.

However, stepping back and gaining a little historical perspective, we see that none of this is new. If you replaced technocrats with the older, accurate, and vaguely more familiar term from ancient Greece—oligarchy—a perspective of much greater value is gained.

We are witnessing the great cycle of political history. After spending a little time thinking about this, the great paleontologist Stephen Jay Gould's sublime book, *Time's Arrow, Time's Cycle* popped into my head. Gould's work is an excellent meditation on the concept of time, borrowing its conceptual framework can help provide some understanding of our present political times.

Gould's book doesn't deal with politics. It is about the idea developed over the past couple of centuries concerning "deep time," the perspective of geologic time, which is still by no means a popular one. This understanding, such that we are actually capable, is that the earth is some five billion years old. Its development allowed for new schools of thought including paleontology, plate tectonics and evolution.

Gould shows the discovery of deep time was made possible by understanding time both in the modern sense of an arrow, that is directional, and simultaneously, in the more ancient sense of time as a cycle. Both were necessary for the human mind to gain perspective on deep time. Gould writes,

"At one end of the dichotomy—I shall call it time's arrow—history is an irreversible sequence of unrepeatable events. Each moment occupies its own distinct position in a temporal series, and all, considered in proper sequence, tell a story of linked events moving in a direction.

"At the other end—I shall call it time's cycle—events have no meaning as distinct episodes with causal impact upon a contingent history. Fundamental states are immanent in time, always present and never changing. Apparent motions are parts of repeating cycles, and differences of the past will be realities of the future. Time has no direction.

"Although both views coexist in this primary document of our culture, we can scarcely doubt that time's arrow is the familiar or "standard" view of most educated Westerners today. This metaphor dominates the Bible itself, and has only increased in strength since then—gaining a special boost from ideas of progress that have attended our scientific and technological revolutions from the seventeenth century onward."

The overwhelming sense of time in modern life is time's arrow. It is embedded in our technology. Looking back, who can argue the computer existed in Renaissance Italy, the automobile in Medieval Europe, or the television in Ancient Rome? Obviously, time has a direction. Time is an arrow, and as Gould points out, it comes with that greatest of modern inventions, the notion of progress.

The perception of time's arrow dominates modern culture, thus it dominates modern politics. It is the domination of the ephemeral at the heart of both popular culture and popular political economy, creating a sense of progress. However, we are witnessing the inability of the ephemeral to meet problems that would better be described as cyclical in nature.

Gould writes,

"Time's arrow of 'just history' marks each moment of time with a distinctive brand. But we cannot, in our quest to understand history, be satisfied only with a mark to recognize each moment and a guide to order events in temporal sequence. Uniqueness is the essence of history, but we also crave some underlying generality, some principles of order transcending the distinction of moments...We also need, in short, the immanence of time's cycle."

How "nature's timeless laws" interact with human history is a question of the greatest importance. Most interestingly, it was the growing knowledge of these laws, and more importantly, human ability to manipulate them, that created everything we deem modern. However, it is important to understand, that as all-encompassing from a historical perspective this manipulation has been in the last two centuries, it is by no means new. It goes back in a more limited, but just as defining way, to the utilization of the first tool.

Gould further explains,

"The metaphor of time's cycle captures those aspects of nature that are either stable or else cycle in simple repeating (or oscillating) series because they are direct products of nature's timeless laws, not the contingent moments of complex historical pathways. The geometry of space regulates how spheres of different sizes may fill a volume in arrangements of regular repetition—and the taxonomy of molecular order in minerals represents a compendium of these possibilities.

"This similarity of time's cycle teaches us something deep about nature's structure because the congruence of ions and tiles is *not* a product of 'just history.' The complex likenesses of organic genealogy are passive retentions from common ancestry—contingencies of historical pathways, not records of immanent regularities. (I type with the same bones used by a bat to fly, a cat to run, and a seal to swim because we all inherited our fingers from a common ancestor, not because laws of nature fashioned these bones independently, and in necessary arrangement.) The complex similarity of tile and mineral patterns records an active, separate development to the same result under immanent rules of natural order."

To say this a little simpler: the world is composed of fundamental elements or forces, whatever way they are used or ordered in any given moment of time to create reality of a certain uniqueness, does not change the fact, that these elements and forces are beneath them all, and are over time unchangeable.

With apologies to Dr. Gould, let's borrow these metaphors for a political perspective, or more accurately a political economy view. From a historical perspective, we understand contemporary uniqueness, but there is no denying that modernity is still composed of fundamental political elements that are unchangeable. The most fundamental of these elements are the characteristics of the species Homo sapiens and the basic survival needs we derive from the planet upon which we evolved. In short, let's say these are, in order of immediacy for survival, air, water, food, reproduction, and defined limits of physical stress.

These are traits humans share with all life, and of course, necessities shared by all members of our species, having not changed in any sense from the great Homo sapiens diaspora out of Africa to the present, now with seven billion habituated across the entire planet. Nor has it changed with the evolution of technology from the spark of the first flint to make fire to the splitting of the atom.

On top of these fundamental Homo sapiens' survival characteristics and interactions with the planet's environment, we have the social component of humanity. As Aristotle opined, "Man is by nature a political animal." It is the processes, methods, and institutions by which we as a social species, a somewhat creative one at that, interact. We call this politics. Our politics allow us as individuals acting collectively to establish systems and technologies providing the fundamental elements necessary for human survival. Politics fostered the creation of technology, which in turn, and particularly under modernity, increasingly defined how we live, that is how we get these basic elements necessary for survival.

Now, let's borrow Gould's metaphors of time's arrow and time's cycle of deep time for an understanding of deep political history. The history of humanity is an arrow in the cycle of the planet. The culture of modernity is an arrow in the cycle of human political history. Understanding the cycle of human political history gives us a much better understanding of the challenges facing us today.

If we look at the whole of human political history, from our development in Africa to the Homo sapiens' diaspora across the rest of the planet, we know very little of its politics. As humanity developed the technology of agriculture and permanent settlements in the last ten thousand years, we begin to know a little more. However, it is not until the development of the ancient civilizations of Mesopotamia and Egypt that we begin to have any real knowledge of the history of Western politics. And, it is in these civilizations, we begin to develop an understanding of time's arrow and time's cycle for politics.

For example, we know the great dynastic periods of Egyptian history, call it Egypt's great arrow, lasted for two thousand years, from around 3000 to 1000 BC. We know in this time there were a series of at least three large peaks and busts. Also, in this two thousand year period, Egypt interacted with the various civilizations of Mesopotamia such as the Sumerians. Finally, we know around the time of 1200 BC, both civilizations would suffer precipitous declines, which the great historian Fernand Braudel describes as, "a recession lasting several centuries and doing so because it corresponded to a particularly stubborn structural crisis."

This general period of decline of these adjacent great civilizations allowed for the relatively brief flourishing of the little kingdom of Israel. More importantly, with this period of decline in the eastern Mediterranean came the establishment further west of the two great interlocking civilizations of Greece and Rome, which in their arrows of time, the Greeks a few hundred years, and the Romans for a thousand years, set the stage for the next thousand and half years of Western politics.

We can say with some, but not much, controversy, that the three thousand year history of Western politics, beginning with the Greeks, has been part of a continuous arrow, comprised of

smaller, shorter arrows, including the Greeks the Romans, Charle-
magne's Holy Roman Empire, the Abbasids, Venice, the Dutch,
French, British, Germans, and the United States.

While one can certainly note the diversity of these cultures, it is
the commonality of the fundamental cyclical political elements for
this discussion that are the most important. Particularly, I'll borrow from the Greek Plato and his determination in *The Republic* of
four distinct categories of conventional political order. They are
timocracy, oligarchy, democracy, and tyranny.

Most have never heard of the first, timocracy, as it was simply a
figment of the Greek's active little imagination, where society is
ruled by the most talented and virtuous—never been such a thing.
What Western history is chock full of is oligarchy—rule of the few,
and tyranny—rule by one. Finally, there is democracy, defined here
simply as rule of the many, and looking across Western history, we
see democracy has been as Gore Vidal noted, an anomaly.

Without getting bogged down into a long and fruitless discussion on defining democracy, particularly opposing what has been
as to what we would like, let's for the purposes of this piece keep it
as rule of the many, or a system in some way for a significant
number to practice "self-government." And again, without getting
bogged down in an argument about how many ruled and who had
self-government, using an historical perspective, comparing the
cultures that we have some sense of over thousand year old Western civilization, the United States of the past two centuries and
post World War II Western Europe, were more democratic than the
vast majority of Western history, and what is in crisis right now, in
both Europe and America, are these democratic systems or what
remains of them. They are overwhelmingly being threatened by a
new oligarchic order—a technocracy—and no doubt, if the descent
is not stopped and reversed, in the not too distant future, some
form of tyranny.

The basic forms of politics rise, combine, separate, and deteriorate to compose the great political cycle. In times when these forms are in movement, the only way to meet the challenges is by recognizing their fundamental cycle character. Of course this is easier said than done, particularly as there are various arrows beginning, in mid-flight, or descending. Our time has some powerful arrows in descent, including the industrial era, hyper-consumptive society, cheap oil, and the Pax Americana, along with equally forceful ascending arrows such as the networked micro-processor.

Any individual human life is an arrow, gaining political meaning only through interactions with the larger cycle. Our culture, institutions, and the design of our environment are the ways through which we gain this meaning. Unfortunately, in both the US and Europe, for the majority of people, the processes, cultures, institutions, the foundational political forces of self-government have become corrupted and deteriorated to the point of meaninglessness. They are only being replaced by the ephemeral sense of time's arrows, causing a destructive nihilism, installing a technocratic monetary oligarchy, seeking further ways to make the majority further indebted, enslaved, and militant—the old tools of every oligarchy.

In such times, it is important to understand what today is described as popular, are the arrows of littlest help. In fact maybe at this time, what will prove to be the least helpful is the electronic—the very nature of electric is ephemeral. Instead, what must be used as a reform foundation for the politics of democracy is the understanding of the cycle, political elements and structures more fundamental than the arrows. The understanding that politics at its root is about power, the cycle of politics defined by how power is distributed.

So, we must look at all the arrow forms and ask how are they democratically composed to get the fundamental needs of Homo sapiens, and then how can a democratic politics be revived, reformed, and evolved. Maybe the most fundamental and immediate issue of our time is an understanding that all the arrows combined since Homo sapiens diaspora out of Africa, have created one large descending arrow in the cycle of humanity's relation to the planet itself.

In order for us to move beyond our present challenges, we need to revisit the past. We need to bring back some old forms unknown to our age, and while they will be shaped by the arrows of our time, the key to political reform is going to be a greater understanding, a renaissance in the understanding of the political cycle.

As Stephen Jay Gould concluded,

"Each of its poles captures, by its essence, a theme so central to intellectual (and practical) life that Western people who hope to understand history must wrestle intimately with both—for time's arrow is the intelligibility of distinct and irreversible events, while time's cycle is the intelligibility of timeless order and lawlike structure. We must have both."

3. ON REPUBLICS

Looking at Western civilization starting around the time of the Ancient Greeks, there are only scattered and relatively short periods of self-government. There were the Greeks and Romans, but after the fall of the Roman republic in the 1st century BC, self-government would disappear from the West for well over a millennium, reappearing briefly in Italy during the Renaissance, in Amsterdam, Switzerland, and in fits and starts in England. It wasn't until the establishment of the American republic two centuries ago, that self-government reasserted itself and not until the 20th century would it become ubiquitous across Europe.

Contemporary Americans have little regard for history. We have an even greater diminishing appreciation for the rarity of self-government, even less appreciation of this inheritance bequeathed us, and a decreasing priority to pass it to future generations. Republics don't collapse abruptly, they are gradually eroded, like Rome. The American republic strains under its military weight and paradoxically its great wealth. Republics don't collapse into anarchy, they shrivel as dispersed power is gradually pulled away from the citizenry and concentrated in centralized government, in the executive.

The only real reform for a republic, as far along the path of decline as the United States is, is to breakup power. Thomas Jefferson was asked how in the last decades of the Roman republic it should have reformed. He replied simply, "Restore independence to all your foreign conquests, relieve Italy from the government of the rabble of Rome, consult it as a nation entitled to self-government, and do its will."

The ability for the United States to undertake such a restoration can only spring from the will of the American people. Yet looking beyond the degradation of America's institutions, we see the republic as a sensibility has declined amongst the people themselves.

Political culture defines the political health of the people; the culture's decline leads way to the government's. A few years ago, HBO had an entertaining and educational series called *Rome*, about the last decades of the Roman republic. In one scene (starts 4:20), they did an exceptional job of simply putting forth the idea of popular decline. In the middle of his war with Octavian, Marc Antony is lulling around Egypt smoking opium and bedding Cleopatra. At this point, Rome is a stinking cesspool. Dressed in Egyptian garb and wearing eyeliner, he gets a message from Octavian taunting him as a coward. Furious and with no self-knowledge of his very un-Roman environment, Antony demands an opinion of his cowardice from Lucius, his chief military-aid.

Lucius, who in the series represents Rome's old republican virtues, replies Antony is no coward but, "You do have a strong disease in your soul. A disease that will eat away at you until you die."

Antony replies, "Really, what is this is disease?"

Lucius, "I'm not a doctor. But, I recognize your symptoms. I have the same sickness."

We Americans have the same disease and we all must fight against it. The only cure is democratic political participation. These processes are the cornerstone of our experience and they must be regular features of our daily lives.

* * *

The degeneration of equality is the most fatal disease of any republic, the disease of consolidating power as Montesquieu points out. It infests the American political system, from our concentrating too much power in Washington DC and a degenerate focus on the whims of the presidency, to the increasing wrongheadedness of meeting all problems by centralizing decision-making. Just as importantly, the consolidation of government power is a symptom of concentrating economic power and the financialization of the economy.

The foundational architecture of democratic political economy of the Roman republic was the yeoman farmer. In his *History of Rome*, Theodor Mommsen does an excellent job describing the republic's destruction through consolidation and financialization:

"In agriculture we have already seen that the growing power of Roman capital was gradually absorbing the intermediate and small landed estates in Italy as well as in the provinces, as the sun sucks up the drops of rain. The government not only looked on without preventing, but even promoted this injurious division of the soil by particular measures... In the provinces, not even the smallest effort was made to save the farmer class there from being bought out by the Roman speculators; the provincials, forsooth, were merely men, and not a party. The consequence was, that even the rents of the soil beyond Italy flowed more and more to Rome. Moreover the plantation-system, which about the middle of this epoch had already gained the ascendant even in particular districts of Italy, such as Etruria, had, through the co-operation of an energetic and methodical management and abundant pecuniary resources, attained to a state of high prosperity after its kind."

By the end of the republic, the distributed independent yeoman farmer was a thing of the past, replaced by the centralized slave plantation, which in turn led to the increasing power of finance. Capital became ever more concentrated, increasingly corrupting government. Mommsen writes,

"The most brilliant, or rather the only brilliant, side of Roman private economics was money-dealing and commerce...The co-operation of rude economic conditions and of the unscrupulous employment of Rome's political ascendancy for the benefit of the private interests of every wealthy Roman rendered a usurious system of interest universal, as is shown for example by the treatment of the war-tax imposed by Sulla on the province of Asia, which the Roman capitalists advanced; it swelled with paid and unpaid interest within fourteen years to sixfold its original amount."

Mommsen sums up Rome's disease,

"Putting together these phenomena, we recognize as the most prominent feature in the private economy of this epoch the financial oligarchy of Roman capitalists standing alongside of, and on a par with, the political oligarchy. In their hands were united the rents of the soil of almost all Italy and of the best portions of the provincial territory, the proceeds at usury of the capital monopolized by them the commercial gain from the whole empire... It is likewise no wonder, that this capitalist oligarchy engaged in earnest and often victorious competition with the oligarchy of the nobles in internal politics. But it is also no wonder, that ruined men of wealth put themselves at the head of bands of revolted slaves, and rudely reminded the public that the transition is easy from the haunts of fashionable debauchery to the robber's cave. It is no wonder, that that financial tower of Babel, with its foundation not purely economic but borrowed from the political ascendancy of Rome, tottered at every serious political crisis..."

This disease that infested the last decades of the Roman republic is not yet quite as advanced in ours. But its symptoms are manifest and obvious for all who care to see. Part of the treatment is to begin breaking up power, the power concentrated in Washington DC, and in our modern-day plantations—the mega-corporations.

As an advantage, we have both Rome's story and the developing understanding order can be provided through distributed power. In fact, this is the architecture of democracy. Unfortunately, Rome's story is lost to our age, while the understanding of distributed political and economic power, using the technologies of the 21st century, is in its infancy. Yet, this should not stop us. We can all learn Rome's tragic tale and though we have a limited culture of distributed power, we can nonetheless begin the breaking-up of concentrated power. Such an endeavor will enthuse our political culture with a needed healthy challenge and revive the Ancient Greeks' wisdom that *archein*, "to begin," is the true freedom of any culture, of any person.

* * *

"The laws of Rome had wisely divided public power among a large number of magistracies, which supported, checked and tempered each other. Since they all had only limited power, every citizen was qualified for them, and the people—seeing many persons pass before them one after the other—did not grow accustomed to any in particular. But in these times the system of the republic changed. Through the people the most powerful men gave themselves extraordinary commissions—which destroyed the authority of the people and magistrates and placed all great matters in the hands of one man or a few." —Montesquieu, *Considerations on the Causes of the Greatness of the Romans and Their Decline*

When reading the history of the bloody and tragic last decades of the Roman republic, one always wants to shout, "Can't you see what's happening? This can be avoided!" Of course to no avail. But in another time and of another republic, when one sees the same diseases infesting the United States, one can only think, "We don't have to do this."

4. CORPORATISM

"This Court now concludes that independent expenditures, including those made by corporations, do not give rise to corruption or the appearance of corruption. That speakers may have influence over or access to elected officials does not mean that those officials are corrupt." —Supreme Court of the United States, Citizens United v. Federal Election Commission

This might be the biggest punch line in the Court's chock-full of laughs decision removing the already limited restraints on corporate control of the election process. Never has the First Amendment to the United States Constitution been wielded so low, in service of the few trampling on the rights of the many. But that's what the Court's for, isn't it?

The public has heard a lot of wailing from good government and campaign finance folks, but really, the Court probably did us all a favor. It removed the ruse. All you have to do is peruse Open Secrets for a few minutes to see how pervasive and powerful corporate money is in our political process. Or as Justice Stevens noted in his worth reading dissent,

"So let us be clear: Neither *Austin* nor *McConnell* held or implied that corporations may be silenced; the FEC is not a 'censor'; and in the years since these cases were decided, corporations have continued to play a major role in the national dialogue."

Over the course of the last century, pretty much every effort to rein in corporate power has been a dismal failure. Today, political and economic power is concentrated in mega-corporations to an extent not reached even at the height of the Gilded Age. And the Supreme Court, more than any other government institution, has both helped create and protect corporate power. The *Citizens United* decision certainly has much Court precedent.

This republic and the modern corporate structure were birthed in the same era, and through the years, at very best, conducted an uneasy relationship. At the dawn of the first Gilded Age, the great grandsons of John Adams, America's second president, Henry and Charles Adams, warned in their book *Chapters of Erie*,

"And yet already our great corporations are fast emancipating themselves from the State, or rather subjecting the State to their own control, while individual capitalists, who long ago abandoned the attempt to compete with them, will next seek to control them. In this dangerous path of centralization Vanderbilt has taken the latest step in advance. He has combined the natural power of the individual with the factitious power of the corporation. The famous "L'Etat, c'est moi" of Louis XIV represents Vanderbilt's position in regard to his railroads. Unconsciously he has introduced Caesarism into corporate life. He has, however, but pointed out the way which others will tread. The individual will hereafter be engrafted on the corporation, democracy running its course, and resulting in imperialism; and Vanderbilt is but the precursor of a class of men who will wield within the State a power created by the State, but too great for its control. He is the founder of a dynasty."

In fits and phases over the next 150 years, the republic tried to address the questions of corporate power, though never with much success. The main obstacle being the question of corporate power requires a fundamental grappling with the basic structures of power. These are questions that for the most part we have strenuously avoided for decades, while corporations increasingly gained enough power to stifle debate.

The real underlying question of corporate power has to do with fundamental political physics. Power is like gravity, it attracts. Once you create a mass of power, such as a giant corporation, it automatically begins attracting all the power around it. The only way to stop this is by breaking it up. This was understood a hundred years ago in the anti-trust debates and the thinking of such people as Louis Brandeis. It was the wisdom of the old republic. Democracy, any self-government, as Thomas Jefferson understood, is inherently decentralized. Yet this knowledge was lost, and no more so with the implementation of the New Deal, which tested the assertion that the power of corporations could be checked and balanced by an equal and opposite governmental force. But anyone without doctrinaire blinders can now clearly see this approach failed—the corporations took over the government.

The Court's decision allows us to have a more fundamental debate, one where the power of our mega-corporations is put front and center. This debate gets to fundamental issues of power across our society, and thus to the question of government itself. The Constitution of the United States was once a radical and visionary document for implementing self-government. After 200 years, it is now increasingly used to thwart those very ends.

* * *

"Some men look at constitutions with sanctimonious reverence and deem them like the ark of the covenant, too sacred to be touched. They ascribe to the men of the preceding age a wisdom

more than human, and suppose what they did beyond amendment... I am certainly not an advocate for frequent and untried
changes in laws and constitutions... But I know also that laws
and constitutions must go hand in hand with the progress of the
human mind... As new discoveries are made, new truths dis-
closed, and manners and opinions change with the change of
circumstances, institutions must advance also, and keep pace
with the times. We might as well require a man to wear still the
coat which fitted him when a boy, as civilized society to remain
under the regimen of their barbarous ancestors... Each generation...has a right to choose for itself the form of government it
believes the most promotive of its own happiness." —Thomas
Jefferson, 1816

* * *

"Both liberty and democracy are seriously threatened by the
growth of big business. Today the need is not so much for freedom from physical restraint as for freedom from economic oppression. Already the displacement of the small independent
businessman by the huge corporation with its myriad of employees, its absentee ownership, and its financier control,
presents a grave danger to our democracy. The social loss is
great; and there is no economic gain. Political liberty, then, is
not enough; it must be attended by economic and industrial liberty.

"There is no such thing as freedom for a man who under normal
conditions is not financially free. We must therefore find means
to create in the individual financial independence against sickness, accidents, unemployment, old age, and the dread of leaving his family destitute, if he suffers premature death. For we
have become practically, a world of employees; and, if a man is

to have real freedom of contract in dealing with his employer, he must be financially independent of these ordinary contingencies. Unless we protect him from this oppression, it is foolish to call him free." —Louis Brandeis

At its inception, our contemporary Tea Party voiced important and legitimate concerns about the bank bailouts and the power of corporations in America. Yet today, both in the corporate media's coverage and the rhetoric of the movement's self-proclaimed representatives, little is being heard concerning the unchecked power of corporations.

That wasn't the case with the Party's revolutionary era ancestors. That Tea Party understood implicitly the tea they were throwing into the Boston Harbor belonged to the East India Company, not the crown. In Nick Robins' excellent history of the East India Company, *The Corporation That Changed the World*, he writes how the American colonial press was filled with vitriol against the East India Company, which the English crown had given monopoly control of the tea trade. Robins writes,

> "From October onwards, newspapers, and handbills provided the citizens of the 13 colonies with a barrage of analysis and polemic. The *Boston Evening Post* of 18 October 1773, for example, contained a powerful article from 'Reclusus' exposing the folly of Lord North's plan. "Though the first Teas may be sold at a low rate to make a popular entry" he acknowledged, "yet when this mode of receiving tea is well established, they, as all other Monopolists do, will mediate a greater profit on their goods, and set them at what price they please."

Lord North's plan was an attempt by the crown to lessen the unpopular taxes, but it was met with more opposition than the original Stamp Act of eight years before. Robins adds another colonist's critique of the Company,

"Writing in *The Alarm* newsletter, 'Rusitcus' underlined how 'their conduct in Asia for some years past, has given simple proof, how little they regard the laws of nations, the rights, liberties, or lives of men'. 'They have levied War, for the sake of gain,' adding: 'fifteen hundred thousands, it is said, perished by famine in one year, not because the earth denied its fruits, but this company and their servants engulfed all the necessities of life, and set them at so high a rate that the poor could not purchase them.'"

As Robins points out, the colonials' actions against the Company preceding the Tea Party had been so highly effective that, "Legal imports of the Company's tea plummeted from a record 869,000 lb in 1768 to just 108,000 lb in 1770."

It's an interesting fact that the American colonials' important and vivid critiques and opposition to the power of the East India Company have mostly been lost to history, as has the history of the Company itself. Both are relevant to our age and to anyone concerned with present questions of freedom, liberty, and democracy. The East India Company set the precedent and became the model for the global mega-corporation of our age, in both its productivity and corruption, and in its completely anti-democratic structures and behaviors. The East India Company existed for over two and half centuries. In that time, with and without the help of the English government, the Company gained monopoly control over Asian trade, conquered and impoverished vast chunks of India causing the largest famine of India's history, and fought two wars with China to keep the illegal and despicable opium trade open, enslaving millions of Chinese.

The East India Company was so notorious in its day they gained the opposition of Adam Smith, Edmund Burke, and Karl Marx. Not exactly an historical coalition that would spring quickly to anyone's mind. Edmund Burke, one of the patron saints of American conservatism, would lead the prosecution in the English parliament for six years in a case against the head of the Company. Burke and his partner Richard Brinsley Sheridan charged,

> "Compared Hastings (the Company's chairman) to the 'writhing obliquity of the serpent' and damned him for a character that was all 'shuffling, ambiguous, dark, insidious, and little'. And as for the Company, it combined 'the meanness of a pedlar and the profligacy of pirates...wielding a truncheon with one hand, and picking a pocket with the other.'"

While Adam Smith, the tremendously misinterpreted and wrongly deified advocate of modern mega-corporate power wrote of the Company,

> "The result of this anti-competitive behavior was to raise profits above the natural level, amounting to (Smith writes) 'an absurd tax upon the rest of their fellow citizens.' Cartels are thus an ever present danger in a market economy and in Smith's immortal words, 'people of the same trade seldom meet together, but the conversation ends in conspiracy against the public or in some contrivance to raise prices.'"

An absurd tax on the rest of us! What can better describe the control of the American economy by the descendants of the East India Company, our own era's global mega-corporations? Robins informs about our present economy, "Over 60 percent of international commerce now takes place within corporations rather than in the open marketplace, making it idle to talk of free markets."

Sounding as relevant today as two centuries ago, Robins describes the Company's operations,

> "It was the speculative behavior of corporate insiders and short-term investors that emerged as the most powerful factor in the

Company's spectacular fall from grace in the middle of the 18th century. Financial engineering, flimsy managerial controls and inadequate regulation all played their part...the same passion for aggressive acquisitions, the same obsession with executive perks for corporate insiders, and the same focus on executive self-preservation as ordinary shareholders started to suffer the consequences of excess."

And what did this financial engineering, inadequate regulation, and corporate insiderism lead to? Repeated bailouts by the government, with the largest occurring at the end of the 18th century. Robins writes,

"To avoid a run on the stock, (Prime Minister) Pitt pushed through legislation extending the Company's ability to raise debt, and so pay its regular dividend at 8 percent. Of course, this measure made little financial sense as the Company was paying dividends out of debt. But it helped to stabilize the situation."

Sound familiar?

The English government, a monarchy, chartered the East India Company, thus the Company had plenty of monarchical characteristics. Modern US mega-corporations are also charted by government, though, with what at this point can only be called a quirk of history, they are chartered through our state governments. With this chartering through the states, it was hoped corporations might be more functionally democratic, but that has not proven the case.

The East India Company still had a relatively small grip on the overall British economy. We live in a time with not one dominant corporation but in an economy completely dominated by several hundred massive corporate structures, riddled with corruption, insiderism and speculation, to such a degree that their "absurd tax" on the rest of us dwarfs the taxes of DC.

Yet, there is no American politics against "oppressive" corporate power. Both parties are completely in the pockets of the corporate oligarchy and if these were or are concerns expressed by the present Tea Party, they've been completely censored by the corporate media and the loathsomely decadent Republican political class.

At the beginning of the 21st century, we can, like this republic's founding generation, step-up to talk about and take action concerning our corrupted and dysfunctional political system. It must include all aspects of power, and that includes the enormous power of the modern global mega-corporation. We would do well to follow the founding America tradition—the first step to dealing with unaccountable power is to break it up. This is the tradition set by the colonial Tea Party and a necessity for self-government. Our present Tea Party might find it useful to go back and read more of America's founding documents, the newspapers, letters, and pamphlets written in the years leading to the Revolution. They would find the founders, not just those in the pantheon, but the thousands scattered up and down the eastern seaboard, had as much concern about the unaccountable power of the nascent corporation as they did of their ancient King.

II. BANKS AND FINANCE

1. FINANCIAL INNOVATION/PONZI FINANCE

The American economy has undergone a dramatic shift over the past three decades, call it the financialization of the US economy. This has been disastrous for the overall political economy, central-izing power and gain in a very small segment of society. Wall Street has gained greater control over every aspect of Americans' daily lives by indebting the nation. A free people are never an in-debted people. It raises great problems for the future.

The financialization of the American economy was birthed in the 1980s, gaining speed in the 90s, and reaching hyper-velocity in the first decade of the 21st century. If one wanted to pick a some-what arbitrary, though nonetheless significant starting point, it would be in 1980, when the Congress removed usury laws control-ling interest rates. The removal of the usury laws gave a flashing green light to the financial sector that more money could be made simply on money. This led to the increasing promotion of debt, along with the infamous financial innovations initiated over the next couple decades, culminating with the destruction of financial regulation in place since the 1930s New Deal.

Financialization is a money game, adding little, though more accurately, no value to the real economy. It distorts the accounting of real value. Most importantly, it is simply a private tax on the rest of society for the profit of a small oligarchy. The true costs hidden until the system is inevitably forced into crisis.

The financialization numbers are simply staggering. In 1950, manufacturing represented 30% of the US economy. Today it is down to 8%. At the same time, the financial sector rose from 10% of the economy to 20%. Even more shocking, corporate profits for the entire financial sector, including insurance and real estate, went from 10% of the economy to 45%, while manufacturing profits dropped to 8%. (Kevin Phillips, *Bad Money*)

In short, financialization is the creation of debt, and boy did Wall Street create debt! As wages stagnated, US household indebtedness rose from $2 trillion dollars in 1984 to $13 trillion twenty years later. The last leg of financialization was the housing market. Mortgage loans went from 30% of bank loans in 1985 to 65% in 2005.

With so much money flooding the system, Wall Street, being the clever folks they are, grabbed the opportunity to make more money on money using "financial innovation." Two of the greatest of these innovations are securitization and derivatives. Securitization takes existing debt, piling it into new debt products so it can be sold again. The other great innovation was derivatives, which are simply bets placed on all existing debt and financial transactions. You don't need a stake in the debt or transaction to place a bet, a true casino, where the house—Wall Street—makes money on each bet.

The FDIC reports annual mortgage securitization went from $110 billion in 1985 to $2.7 trillion in 2005. Meanwhile, the Bank for International Settlements states in 2008, derivatives represented $684 trillion in positions, on a global economy of $60 trillion. In this quarter-century of exponential growth, debt, depending on which sectors you choose, expanded by factors of anywhere from the tens to hundreds, while the US economy grew only 2.5 times larger, though this is a misleading figure as it accounts for much, but not all of the financial bubble. What financialization has created is a massive money bubble on top of the real economy, which for various reasons doesn't filter completely into the real economy. As John Maynard Keynes wrote,

> "But the volume of trading in financial instruments, i.e. the activity of financial business, is not only highly variable but has no close connection with the volume of output whether of capital goods or of consumption-goods."

Total debt in the US is somewhere over $50 trillion, which means compared to fifty years ago where each 1.5 dollar of debt represented a dollar of economic activity, it is now close to five dollars of debt for each dollar of activity. Greater debt is a burden for the vast majority of the economy. The resulting massive profits are realized by only a few. Today, six institutions account for over 60% of the financial industry, which taken together means a concentration of financial power unprecedented in American history.

With the panic of the financial elite in the fall of 2008, trillions of dollars of private debt, through the agency of the Fed, Treasury, and Fannie/Freddie were transferred onto the public books. In addition, the public sector created massive new debt in response to a cataclysmic deflation, adding to the overall debt burden. Still, there remains a tremendous amount of worthless debt, unaccounted losses, or dead money on bank books, government books and across the entire economy, which will continue to hinder and distort all future economic activity.

* * *

"When you see reference to a new financial paradigm you should always, under all circumstances, take cover. Because ever since the great tulipmania in 1637, speculation has always been covered by a new paradigm." —John Kenneth Galbraith

A classic Ponzi scheme always needs new money. Once new money stops flowing, the con collapses. In 2008, just as in any good Ponzi scheme, once the new money (the liquidity) dried up, the whole thing began collapsing. So the Federal Reserve System, the planet's leading liquidity/new money provider stepped in, providing trillions of dollars of liquidity. There's a thin line between the healthiest banking system and a Ponzi effort, and this line was obliterated with Wall Street's and the big banks' financial innovations. The Fed's unprecedented and extraordinary liquidity flows of the last several years in essence make the American taxpayer the last pocket in the Great Global Ponzi Finance Con.

We now have a system addicted to liquidity. This liquidity allows continued payment on bad debt, keeping inflated severely distorted prices of debt, equity, and commodities. Excess liquidity is detrimental to both the financial system and the real economy. With the pricing system distorted, you get plenty of malinvestments, simply investments that should never be made. It becomes increasingly difficult to distinguish between what might be simple problems of short-term finance vs. major issues of insolvency. If you just keep pumping more and more liquidity into an insolvent entity, you only further distort the economy.

This is the great problem we currently face with the global financial system. The great liquidity bubble has distorted global assets, the real economy, and now is creating problems for currencies. We can't tell what is healthy or solvent, from what is sick or insolvent. It is difficult to tell good debt from bad, thus good money from bad. In Europe, we watch the liquidity pushers trying to solve the problems caused by excess liquidity with more liquidity, once again revealing the underlying Ponzi nature of the system. The United States is the largest liquidity pusher, the Fed the greatest culprit. With the dollar as the global reserve currency, this has exasperated the Ponzi bubble across the globe.

The Bank of International Settlements has an excellent report, showing just how reliant the Europeans remain on the dollar. Meaning, in times of crisis such as 2008 and now, Europe desperately needs the US Fed. So much for the Euro. BIS states:

> "The funding difficulties which arose during the crisis are directly linked to the remarkable expansion in banks' global balance sheets over the past decade. Reflecting in part the rapid pace of financial innovation, banks' (particularly European banks') foreign positions have surged since 2000...European banks' need for short-term US dollar funding was substantial at the onset of the crisis, at least $1.0–1.2 trillion by mid-2007.

> "Events during the crisis led to severe disruptions in banks' sources of short-term funding. Interbank markets seized up, and dislocations in FX swap markets made it even more expensive to obtain US dollars via swaps."

The most amazing statement in the BIS report about the banks piling on debt is, "The associated currency exposures were presumably hedged off-balance sheet." Hedging, derivatives, and the idea of "investing insurance" are all the final and essential components of the Great Global Ponzi Financial Con, all the more ludicrous as the processes themselves make the system more unstable. It misleads all into thinking that no one needs to take losses, and that folks is Ponzi thinking!

The question is how to end the Great Global Ponzi Finance Con. Two things need to be done and they must be done simultaneously. First, the financial industry needs to be shrunk by at least half, and the best way to do that is to drain the liquidity out of the system. This means making things less liquid—less trade-able—a greater reliance on long-term opposed to short-term finance, much less if any securitization, and finally an ending of the too prevalent practices of hedging and derivatives. We are doing none of this.

Secondly, the system must be brought into account, meaning a lot of bad debt needs to be destroyed. This will be deflationary, but the way to mitigate the impact is as money is destroyed in the Ponzi system, pump more directly into the real economy, keeping people employed and beginning to invest in the future.

* * *

If you've spent much time in the less industrial areas of this planet, you almost inevitably end up with some kind of parasite. When they infest your intestinal tract, you suddenly become well aware of just how important this system is to your body. Now some parasites run their course fairly quickly, while others can linger for years. Many otherwise healthy organisms can live with parasites for a long time, but particularly virulent types will eventually kill. Our financial system, the intestinal system of our economy, is infested with parasites. They brought the global economy to its knees and continue actively feeding and multiplying in their host. If we do not rid our system of these parasites, they will eventually bring us down.

A couple years ago, a great book on our financial parasites was released, Kevin Phillips' Bad Money. Phillips diagnoses the problem,

"Without much publicity, the financial services sector—banks, broker-dealers, consumer finance, insurance, and mortgage finance—muscled past manufacturing in the 1990s to become the largest sector of the US private economy. By 2004-6, financial services represented 20 to 21 percent of gross domestic product, manufacturing just 12 to 13 percent."

Our economy became infested with parasites living off the host, and one might add, living quite well. We need to rid our economic body of the parasites. We can cut the size of our financial sector in half at least. We can remove the middleman of Wall Street out of public money creation and retie investors directly to their investments. We can get rid of the notion that risk is avoidable. Investors need to be directly responsible for losses, just as they directly benefit from profit. Unfortunately, the process to do this is broken. One of the great problems of our parasite infestation is they formed a symbiotic relationship with the host's defense mechanisms—our elected officials. The American economy will not get back to health into we rid ourselves of this parasite infestation. We will not be able to do that until we revive the health of our politics.

* * *

"The result has been a massive transfer of wealth, with its centerpiece the greatest theft from the public purse in history. This campaign has been far too consistent and calculated to brand it with the traditional label, "spin". This manipulation of public perception can only be called *propaganda*. Only when we, the public, are able to call the underlying realities by their proper names—extortion, capture, looting, propaganda—can we begin to root them out." —Yves Smith, *Econned*

When we dropped political from economy, we made a grave and what might prove fatal error. We made the republic subservient to mega—corporations and allowed the dominance of crackpot pop-economic theories to trample over the millenia-old hard won wisdom of self-government. For example, how many economic theories have been written on the importance of the First Amendment's freedom of the press to the vitality of the American political economy—not many, if even one?

Yet, a vigorous free press is essential to every aspect of American prosperity. So, as our newspapers folded and consolidated and our broadcast media became handmaidens to corporate power, we witnessed a tremendous decline in journalism, particularly investigative journalism, which had a long and important tradition in this republic's vitality. The mother of investigative journalism, particularly concerning corporate power, is Ida Tarbell, who a century ago wrote, *The History of the Standard Oil Company*, documenting the manipulations, thefts, grafts, and other criminal activities of John D. Rockefeller and his cohorts in their monopolization of the oil industry.

While we have lost the great tradition of a hearty journalism in our old media, it is rising again across the new medium of the Internet, and it has been utilized in helping shed light on the underlying scandal of the financial crisis. In the tradition of hard hitting, no bullshit investigation, Yves Smith has written Econned: How Unenlightened Self Interest Undermined Democracy and Corrupted Capitalism.

Econned is the story of how our financial system has become a mass ruse, allowing Wall Street and the largest banks to become predatory, treating their clients as lambs to be fleeced and fatted calves to be slaughtered. It is the story of how a very small group of people gained complete control over the American, and much of the global economy, driving it into the ground, then walking away with trillions of more dollars, while the economy remains on life-support.

How did this happen? *Econned* tells the story, starting with the greatest problem of contemporary economics, an economics stripped of politics, so it might pretend to be a science. Smith goes through the litany chanted by our economic priesthood for the past several decades—efficient market theory, free markets, and mathematically modeling the future—the equivalent of economic hokum that allowed Wall Street and the banks to dismantle New Deal regulations which kept their worst abuses in check for a half-century.

Once establishing the intellectual foundations, Smith explains the great scaffolding of fraud erected on top of it. She documents the roles of Bankers Trust, Salomon Brothers, JP Morgan, Citi and others as they "innovated" their way out of regulation and into their clients' pockets with derivatives, securitization, and other "efficiencies." All along, right beside them, stood our elected officials and regulators, such as Fed Chiefs Greenspan and Bernanke, Treasury Secretaries Baker, Rubin, Summers, and Paulson, SEC chiefs, congress people, and presidents—all co-conspirators.

In the final third of the book, Smith details the pinnacle of the great con and how it all came crashing down. Then, the government stepped in to help an orderly looting of the public purse worth trillions of dollars and counting, thus insuring a crippled economy for many years to come.

Econned is an excellent read and should be read by all. It is the story of a criminal class, who has separated themselves from the majority to seek their own profits. It is the story of how our political economy is broken. In the end, it is a call to the American people, in the great tradition of this republic, to step-up and fix it. Yves Smith is a citizen and patriot, she deserves our gratitude.

* * *

"FUNDAMENTAL BASIS OF A CULTURE OF TRADERS.—We have now an opportunity of watching the manifold growth of the culture of a society of which commerce is the soul, just as personal rivalry was the soul of culture among the ancient Greeks, and war, conquest, and law among the ancient Romans. The tradesman is able to value everything without producing it, and to value it according to the requirements of the consumer rather than his own personal needs. "How many and what class of people will consume this?" is his question of questions. Hence, he instinctively and incessantly employs this mode of valuation and applies it to everything, including the productions of art and science, and of thinkers, scholars, artists, statesmen, nations, political parties, and even entire ages: with respect to everything produced or created he inquires into the supply and demand in order to estimate for himself the value of a thing. This, when once it has been made the principle of an entire culture, worked out to its most minute and subtle details, and imposed upon every kind of will and knowledge, this is what you men of the coming century will be proud of—if the prophets of the commercial classes are right in putting that century into your possession! But I have little belief in these prophets." — Friedrich Nietzsche, *Daybreak: Reflections on Moral Prejudice*

2. THE FED/BANKS

"You could not step twice into the same river; for other waters are ever flowing on to you." —Heraclitus of Ephesus

Liaquat Ahamed's *Lords of Finance* is an excellent read on the financial predicaments of the 1920s. Though we face different circumstances today, Ahamed's history of the era offers much understanding on how we got here, providing valuable knowledge on where we need to go.

Lords of Finance focuses on the four men who ran the central banks of the United States, Britain, France, and Germany in an era of great financial turbulence leading to the Great Depression. It is an excellent popular history, painting a wonderful picture of the era and of those who helped, for better and worse, to define it. It also does a good job of laying forth the financial conundrum in a way people can understand.

Mr. Ahamed's main contention is that the gold standard was the culprit behind the currency turbulence of the 1920s. However, I think the story he tells leads to a little different conclusion. Debt was really the main problem and the gold standard both a catalyst aggravating the situation and a hindrance in developing solutions. The end of WWI saw a much different world than the beginning, especially in the financial sector. Most important, three of Europe's great powers became indebted to each other and the newly developing American financial colossus, representing a shift in underlying economic power that would cause havoc for the next ten years. Ahamed writes,

> "They burdened a world of economy still trying to recover from the effects of war with gigantic overhang of international debts. Germany began the 1920s owing some $12 billion in reparations to France and Great Britain; France owed the United States and Britain $7 billion in war debts, while Britain in turn owned $4 billion to the United States. This would be the equivalent today of Germany owing $2.4 trillion, France $1.4 trillion, and Britain owing $800 billion. Dealing with these massive claims consumed the energies of financial statesman for much of the decade and poisoned international relations. More important, the debts left massive fault lines in the world financial system, which cracked at the first pressure."

In his 1919 seminal The Economic Consequences of the Peace, John Maynard Keynes wrote the war debt, particularly the punitive reparations placed on the Germans, would lead to economic calamity. Over the course of the next decade, Germany, Britain and France would scramble to keep this debt from crippling their domestic economies and exports. The debt led to continuous currency volatility, including Germany's hyperinflation of the early 1920s and finally the collapse of the entire system by the end of the decade.

Lords of Finance is the story of the constant interaction between the four nations' central banks and their attempts to create a stable currency situation, with the United States playing the role of lender of last resort. Mr. Ahamed shows how sticking to the gold standard aggravated the situation and getting off the gold standard eventually alleviated some of the problems. However, the debt and underlying real economy imbalances in the system would take a decade and half and another world war to come to resolution.

The gold standard was not so much a cause of the currency destabilization as a catalyst. It forced more frequent and severe valuations and revaluations then was necessary. Gold is an anti-inflationary money base and inflation is finance's worst enemy. All debt loses value with inflation, thus if you want the money you lent back, you want to keep inflation at a minimum. The natural scarcity of gold can help curb, but not prevent inflation.

This is important for understanding the present global economic predicament. The question of debt, not just in the US, but in Greece and other nations across Europe is leading the news. Yet, even without the gold standard, debt is causing increasing turbulence in currency markets. Our modern lords of finance are just as fearful of inflation as their predecessors were, and while they don't have gold, they have the Euro, derivatives and other financial innovations as a catalyst. They are fearful of losing their money. They are slowly turning the screws on many nations to create no more debt and pay what they owe. The debt and increasing volatility are beginning to jam the wheels of commerce.

The debt problem of today is exponentially larger than the 1920s. In the past decades, we have added layer upon layer of "innovative debt" on top of more traditional debt. Advocating more debt, without getting rid of existing debt, will slowly strangle the future. Mr. Keynes understood this better than his disciples.

Just as after WWI, present debt and currency volatility are pointing to underlying real economy imbalances. Unlike in the 1920s, the United States is not the planet's largest creditor, it is the largest debtor, yet it still plays the role of lender of last resort. Ahamed writes of the 1920s,

"Eventually the policy of keeping US interest rates low to shore up the international exchanges precipitated a bubble in the US stock market."

Today, Mr. Bernanke keeps interest rates low and pumps up not only the US stock market, but creates new bubbles across the globe. Neither this nor the debt ocean created in the last thirty years is sustainable.

We have new lords of finance. While the Fed remains powerful, debt has grown to such a degree to make it less so. Over the years, the Fed has ceded power to our new lords of finance on Wall Street and to the mega-banks, who have created more debt in the last several decades than the world has seen in all its previous history. At some point, just as the WWI war reparations and war debt was written down or off, we are going to have to do the same. Recently, there was a half attempt at this with Greece. We need to dethrone the new lords of finance and place the real economy, in all its diversity and concreteness, in charge. We need to bring this queer thing known as money down from the marble palaces and into the democratic assembly.

* * *

In reading some economic material on the Depression of the 1930s, trying to figure out what Fed Chair Bernanke's bet of the dollar means for the global economy, I began to worry my memory was faulty, an occurrence of greater frequency these days. However, I discovered on this matter, it wasn't my memory. Instead, I discovered "revisionist history" had occurred, and this makes me even more nervous about Ben's Bet.

I researched the "beggar thy neighbor" policies of the 1930s where countries enacted trade tariffs, import restrictions, and currency depreciation in the fight against economic contraction. In the early 1930s, a number of countries raced to devalue their currencies for export advantage, only aggravating global deflationary movements. However, I found Micheal Pettis, who has some interesting insights on China, had linked to a paper being touted by the National Bureau of Economic Research entitled, "The Roots of Protectionism." The abstract states,

> "Thus, the 1930s' rush to protectionism was not so much a triumph of special-interest politics as it was a result of second-best macroeconomic policies, the authors write. Their study 'suggests that had more countries been willing to abandon the gold standard and use monetary policy to counter the slump, fewer would have been driven to impose trade restrictions.'"

So, there it was. As monetary theory ascended power over the last several decades, history was rewritten or revised accordingly. Currency depreciation moved from the "beggar thy neighbor" problem column, onto the monetary solution part of the ledger—call it neo-double entry accounting. So, I thought, "This is what wily old Ben is thinking." I went and looked up Mr. Bernanke's Essays on the Great Depression, and in Chapter Three (page 78), Mr. Bernanke writes,

> "Eichengreen and Sachs (1985) similarly focused on the beneficial effects of currency depreciation (i.e., abandonment of the gold standard or devaluation). For a sample of ten European countries, they showed that depreciating countries enjoyed faster growth of exports and industrial production, than countries which did not depreciate. Depreciating countries also experienced lower real wages and greater profitability, which presumably helped to increase production. Eichengreen and Sachs argued that depreciation, in this context, should not necessarily be thought of as a "beggar thy neighbor" policy; because depreciations reduce constraints on the growth of world money supplies, they may have conferred benefits abroad as

well as home (although a coordinated depreciation presumably would have been better than the uncoordinated sequence of depreciations that in fact took place)."

Professor Bernanke writes,

"If monetary contraction propagated by the gold standard was the source of the worldwide deflation and depression, then countries abandoning the gold standard (or never adopting it) should have avoided much of the deflationary pressure. This seems to be the case."

"This seems to be the case." Now there's scientific rigor. Why such a hedge? Because data from the 1930s, particularly worldwide, is notoriously sketchy. As Bernanke writes further down, "We included countries for which the League of Nations collected reasonably complete data on industrial production, price levels, and money supplies." Hey-ho, "reasonably complete data," good enough for the science of economics.

Both Professor Eichengreen and Professor Bernanke state the data show countries that abandoned the gold standard, that is depreciated their currencies, were the first to mitigate deflationary problems. First, the data remains at best sketchy to come up with any grand conclusions, and in fact if it is of value, proves "beggar thy neighbor" worked—if you acted first.

Secondly, even if the data is of much value, the Professors, looking to prove the case of a monetary hammer for pounding all economic nails, at best commit the eternal freshman mistake of correlation as causation. The "money shot," so to speak, is Professor Bernanke's conclusion,

"The expected differences in the monetary policies of the gold and non-gold countries seem to be in the data, although somewhat less clearly than we had anticipated."

"In summary, data from our sample of twenty-four countries support the view that there was a strong link between adherence to the gold standard and the severity of both deflation and depression. The data are also consistent with the hypothesis that increased freedom to engage in monetary expansion was a reason for the better performance of countries leaving the gold standard early in the 1930s, although evidence in this case is a bit less clear-cut."

There are the golden words of economics—"seem to be in the data"—and even better, "although the evidence in this case is a bit less clear-cut." Good enough evidence for Chairman Bernanke to bet the dollar like some drunken sailor at the roulette table— "It's been black four times in a row, 'seems to be' red is now inevitable. Bet the wad!" And that's what we're doing.

Now, I'm not making an argument that getting off the gold standard wasn't helpful. What I'm questioning is the value of coordinated global currency deprecation. Mr. Bernanke's monetary policy of depreciating the dollar, classic "beggar thy neighbor," is hurting exporting nations not pegged to the dollar. As the dollar is the equivalent of the gold standard today, we are not depreciating just currency, but the standard itself. Despite all worrying about the dollar, what we are seeing is the Fed Chairman trying to instill his theorized policies prescriptions for the 1930s of "coordinated depreciation." Mr. Bernanke, it would seem, is trying to force currency depreciations across the board to prove his theory "a coordinated depreciation presumably would have been better."

Monetarist theory was behind this financial crisis, a belief in what Professor Eichengreen calls, "the self-equilibrating tendencies of the market." Phew, "self-equilibrating!" In the 1930s that would have been known as a ten-cent word. It is a belief today that has cost tens of trillions of dollars and counting. The financial crisis was proof of the fallacy of much of the theory at the foundation of monetarism and other market theories, the idea it's going to get us out of the mess seems incredulous. We're in the hands of academics trying to bend reality to their theories. Place your bets. Professor Chairman Ben has made his.

3. DEBT AND SOLVENCY

"They have learned nothing and forgotten nothing." —Talley rand on the Bourbon Restoration

In 2010, leading financial journalist Martin Wolf had a piece in the FT getting to the heart of financial matters, while inadvertently showing the insolvency of our economic thinking. In the end, Mr. Wolf's piece is a defense of fiscal spending in reaction to deflation. In so doing, he makes the case, but confusedly, of the importance of understanding the difference between assets and debt. Wolf writes,

> "But the time has come to look at the longer-run implications. This is particularly important when one considers fiscal consoli- dation. On this I make a simple point: it is not just about debt; it must also be about assets."

Mr. Wolf's argument is confused because, at a financial level, debts and assets are in many instances the same thing, accounted for differently in separate ledgers. Mr. Wolf attempts correctly, but not convincingly to offer a little clarification stating,

> "Yet governments should not sacrifice the future to the pressures of the present. What is the sense of cutting spending today if the result is a poorer country tomorrow? This point turns on its head the refrain that we should at all costs avoid burdening the future with additional debt. We should indeed avoid burdening the future with unproductive debt. Yet productive debt is not a burden, but a blessing."

The problem here, and it is a big one, is that matters of finance and money are not integrated into modern economic philosophizing. That Mr. Wolf, who understands finance better than 99% of those writing on economic matters, is maybe confused reveals how conventional thinking on such matters offers little help in extracting us from the problems the world finds itself mired.

The greatest argument for those advocating more fiscal stimulus is there is no inflation, but inflation is not the only symptom of a malfunctioning or dysfunctional financial/monetary/economic system. Insolvency is also an important measure. In a functioning market system, insolvency at the individual and business level is an important mechanism for balancing the system. However, insolvency at industry-wide levels, such as in banking or housing, or at a national level, are signals of much greater problems, problems not simply corrected by pouring in more money.

Mr. Wolf's piece once again ignores, as does almost all modern economic analysis, the problems of financial bubbles. They are first and foremost a problem of the financial/monetary system, and secondly, depending on their size and length, they tremendously distort the underlying real physical economy. In all cases, bubbles are manifestations of unsustainable practices. They create unproduc-

tive debt. Thus, the dichotomy Mr. Wolf addresses between pro-
ductive and unproductive debt is important and key to understanding our future, but more difficult to discern after large bubbles.
Wolf continues, seeming to not really believe the distinction. He
states,

> "Yet, in the short run, with demand below capacity, even bor-
> rowing that raises current consumption would be better than
> leaving resources idle. The fact that some residents (future tax-
> payers) may then have to pay a little more to other residents
> (bondholders) is surely a second order issue."

Much of this "demand below capacity" and "leaving resources
idle" are the result of preceding unsustainable bubbles. Simply attempting to blow them back up is not only impossible, it is detrimental. This is not a matter of "future taxpayers" paying more to
other "resident (bondholders)," it is indenturing the future to a
bankrupt past. With this statement, Mr. Wolf could very well be
accused of being plainly disingenuous, particularly in relation to
the reality of the Irish, where the Irish government, leaving aside
any argument on fiscal policy, is indebting the future to pay off the
bad loans of English and German banks. But it gets worse. Wolf inadvertently reveals the true insolvency of much of our economic
priesthood when he states,

> "Some insist loudly that one cannot solve a problem caused by
> too much debt by piling on more debt. But that is wrong. In the
> US and UK, net debt is close to zero: thus, debt is not a burden
> on society as a whole, but an obligation of some residents to
> others. As Nobel-laureate Paul Krugman points out, debt mat-
> ters only because of who the debtors are. If, for example, debtors
> suffer an unexpected loss in net wealth or are forced suddenly
> to repay, the impact on the economy is bound to be fiercely con-
> tractionary. If the state can borrow, to offset this effect, it should

do so. That would not impose an overall burden on a society, since net debt would remain close to zero. If it also raised GDP above what it would otherwise be, that would surely be a very good thing."

Phew, invoking Krugman and his Nobelness in defense shows without a doubt the lack of needed critical thinking, though it demonstrates the ahistorical thinking of our economic priesthood. First, from a current accounts balance perspective, arguing that US "net debt" is zero is incredulous, accounting gimmickry, something at which we do excel. Second, the question of solvency from a national perspective, concerning what the debt is comprised of, is important for the US, and really who cares about the British? History is littered with nations, Mr. Wolf's old Britannia for one, who continued to add to their debts, a better word being liabilities, in an attempt to sustain the unsustainable, leading eventually to national insolvency. Yet, Mr. Wolf wants to disregard these problems in lieu of the great magic elixir of our industrial capital priesthood, growth, "a raised GDP."

Mr. Wolf is right, the difference between debt and assets is key, but in a system where the accounting of debts and assets is completely confused, in fact where all debt is simply notched as someone's asset, it is problematic. Where a financial system is completely removed from the real economy, combined with a political system that is eminently corrupt, the further wanton dumping of money into the system will only create greater distortions and future hardship. For example, all dumping of money into the US economy furthering our oil addiction, whether it's infrastructure supporting the internal combustion engine or military misadventures across the Mid-East, is not just bad debt, but destructive liabilities, though this might not seem the case to collar counties of Maryland and Virginia.

The problem is the American political economy is so distorted and so corrupt it is not able to tell the difference between good and bad debt. In fact, it favors bad debt. That is why talking about simply dumping more money into the system, without a corresponding discussion of reforming our financial, corporate, political and government systems is not simply detrimental, but destructive. We can begin a healthy discussion on the future in deciding what debt is going to be destroyed and how the losses are going to be accounted. Afterwords, we can have a better understanding what future good debt looks like. Without doing this, all the talk of throwing more money at our problems is nothing more than a desperate attempt by a decadent and corrupt aristocracy and their servants to keep in place a failed status quo.

* * *

Bill Gross' partner at PIMCO, Mohammed El-Erian published an article in the FT provoking thought. Mr. Elan is the voice of the bond kingdom and they are united in one thing, the debt they hold must be made good. After all, that is how the game works, but the bond kingdom has some responsibility for the ocean of garbage debt the world has been flooded with over the past couple decades, thus a responsibility beyond recommendations on how to insure they're paid.

Mr. El-Erian states, and he's right, the Panic of 2008 created a sea change, and no one really yet understands what this means. He suggests:

"Today, we should all be paying attention to a new theme: the simultaneous and significant deterioration in the public finances of many advanced economies. At present this is being viewed primarily—and excessively—through the narrow prism of

Greece. Down the road, it will be recognised for what it is: a significant regime shift in advanced economies with consequential and long-lasting effects."

He then adds:

"The shock to public finances is undermining the analytical relevance of conventional classifications. Consider the old notion of a big divide between advanced and emerging economies. A growing number of the former now have significantly poorer economic and financial prospects, and greater vulnerabilities, than a growing number of the latter."

These ideas are important for several reasons. First, this isn't a situation that developed in the last two years. It has taken several decades to get here. Second, what Mr. El-Erian is describing is the process of corporate globalization, specifically, its impact on older industrial economies. The win-win-win notion of corporate globalization has always been the most vile of propaganda. 6.5 billion people on this planet cannot live like 300 million uber-consumptive Americans. It is a physical impossibility.

Over the past decades, growth in the "developing" world has in many instances been at the cost of the "developed" world. This fact is literally papered-over with debt. The United States is the best and shiniest example of the creation of historic levels of pubic and private debt to obscure the impact of corporate globalization. Of course, it's important to understand this corporate model was built atop a five-centuries-old model of European/American global domination. If you have any sense of fairness, this situation cannot be defended. You cannot, except at the point of a gun, ask the vast majority of people in the world to be economically subservient to the few.

Mr El-Erian points out that it's ridiculous to look at the global economy and suggest one size fits all. The old industrial nations of

Europe, the United States, and Japan do not need the kind of growth of China, India, Africa, or Brazil. At the same time, the models of modernity, the United States and to a lesser extent Europe are simply not transferable to the other six billion people on this planet. We all need to rethink how and for what our economies function.

Mr. El-Erian writes the world is birthing a new era:

"We should expect (rather than be surprised by) damaging recognition lags in both the public and private sectors. Playbooks are not readily available when it comes to new systemic themes. This leads many to revert to backward-looking analytical models, the thrust of which is essentially to assume away the relevance of the new systemic phenomena."

I couldn't be in more agreement. The question is what are these new "systemic phenomena." Mr. El-Erian then writes:

"Here, history suggests that it is not easy for companies and governments to overcome the tyranny of backward-looking internal commitments."

Compare this to what Keynes wrote in 1929 in his *Treatise on Money*,

"I think it is desirable that the obligations arising out of past borrowing, of which National Debts are the most important, should, as time goes on, gradually command less and less of human effort and of the results of human effort; that progress should loosen the grip of the dead hand; that the dead hand should not be allowed to grasp the fruits of improvement long after the live body which once directed it has passed away."

Compare both with Thomas Jefferson's thinking on the matter in a letter to James Madison,

"The question Whether one generation of men has a right to bind another...is a question of such consequences as not only to merit decision, but place also, among the fundamental principles of every government...I set out on this ground which I suppose to be self evident, 'that the earth belongs in usufruct to the living', that the dead have neither powers nor rights over it.

"The received opinion, (is) the public debts of one generation devolve on the next. ...but between society and society, or generation and generation there is no municipal obligation, no umpire but the law of nature. We seem not to have perceived that, by the law of nature, one generation is to another as one independant nation to another."

"But with respect to future debts; would it not be wise and just for that nation to declare in the constitution they are forming that neither the legislature, nor the nation itself can validly contract more debt, than they may pay within their own age, or within the term of 19 years? And that all future contracts shall be deemed void as to what shall remain unpaid at the end of 19 years from their date? This would put the lenders, and the borrowers also, on their guard. By reducing too the faculty of borrowing within its natural limits, it would bridle the spirit of war, to which too free a course has been procured by the inattention of money lenders to this law of nature, that succeeding generations are not responsible for the preceding."

It is quite incorrigible for one generation to bind the next with their debts. As Mr. El-Erian suggests, we are in a new era. It would be despicable via massive debt to chain it to the past. We need to destruct a great deal of this debt, and it must be done to free the future. The future must be allowed to find its own way. The dead hand of the past through gross negligence has lost both moral and fiscal authority.

So, what say you Mr. Gross and Mr. El-Erian? How about a little public service? Explain what sort of haircut you'd be willing to take to help right the ships of state on this sea of change we all embark.

4. JUBILEE: THE POLITICS OF DEFAULT

Jubilee is part of the Judeo/Christian tradition. It is codified in Leviticus one of the great law books of the Torah. And of course, the Christ was the personification of Jubilee, whose birth is perceived as humanity's manumission from sin. A debt Jubilee is a large scale freeing of debtors, and/or as Willem Buiter of the *Financial Times* suggests, a mass scale swap of debt for equity.

America is a massively indebted society. Indebted people are not free. We need to change this. There are a couple of easy things we can do such as loan modifications for underwater homeowners, writing down the principal to present market values, thus lowering monthly payments. Also, a one-time wiping away of student debt for everyone under 35 would be healthy. We need to free them and some of our institutions from their constraining debt load in order to make the changes necessary for a sustainable future. The more we keep shackling people, institutions, and society with debt, the more we are constrained to the status quo and the past. We will make necessary change impossible.

This is the key to establishing a politics of default. It is the only way we're going to free ourselves from our financial oligarchy and begin a real discussion and action to creating an economy for the 21st century. Make no mistake, the continuing creation of more and more debt without destructing the bad debt is enslaving ourselves to failure, each year leaving a growing number of Americans behind.

Debt destruction will have tremendous deflationary impacts, and the government(s) are going to have to respond, adding the additional problem that our government is corrupt and dysfunctional, so along with financial reform, we're going to need political and government reform.

Over time, in order to reorder the American economy, we're going to have to write-off a lot of bad debt, debt owed by business, government, and individuals. This debt represents problems of the economy, trying to make it good only creates more bad money. The more we keep the bad debt in circulation and keep adding bad debt on top of it, the bigger the hole we're digging for ourselves.

In the 1930's, John Maynard Keynes could look at the half-industrialized economies of the United States and Europe and see all sorts of viable industrial economic activity sitting idle for lack of capital. He was right to think this a ridiculous situation. Today, you can look at vast parts of the globe—Asia, Africa, and South America—and for the moment disregarding resource constraints, see all sorts of viable established industrial economic activity that should not be hindered by lack of capital. However, you can't say that for the United States. Creating 50,000 more McDonald's jobs doesn't serve anyone well.

We can't build the future by increasingly indebting ourselves to a failing and increasingly criminal status quo. The first step out of our predicament is destroying the bad debt, because it's creating more and more bad money and this is all creating an increasingly bad politics.

* * *

"It remained clear, however, that unresolved questions about the inherited financial system might well make a sudden and unexpected reappearance if, at any time in the second half of the twentieth century, shifts in world trade and the cost of imported materials place severe forms of competitive pressure on the American economy and on the international monetary system. At such a moment the cultural consolidation fashioned in the Gilded Age would undergo its first sustained re-evaluation, as the "financial question" once again intruded into the nation's politics and issues of Populism again penetrated the American consciousness." —Lawrence Goodwyn, *The Populist Moment*, 1978

III. MONEY

"The process by which banks create money is so simple that the mind is repelled." —John Kenneth Galbraith, *Money: Whence It Came, Where It Went*

Banks create money. Banks create money out of thin air. It's a simple process. They start with a hundred dollars, mark it as an asset, then lend that $100 to someone else, mark that as an asset, and as the French say voila, now the bank has $200. They can then lend another $100 on that, and if they wanted, keep the creation process going to infinity. However, in a fractional reserve system, which supposedly the US banking system is, the bank's money creation process is limited. In a fractional reserve system with 10% reserves, only $90 can be lent out on the first $100, then $81 on the next loan, all down the line to where you can no longer create any new money. A fractional reserve system limits the money creation process. However today, due to financial innovation and creative accounting, this is no longer the case.

Just as importantly, the value of money created by any given bank is based on the value of their loans. Frank Capra had it exactly right when he had Jimmy Stewart telling the customers of Bailey Building and Loans that he didn't have all their money, it was spread across the value of the housing loans. This is important to understanding the workings of any debt money system. Most of the money becomes illiquid, that is, it is not easily transferable, and this provides stability for the monetary system. Call it long-term solid money—mortgages, business loans, and bonds.

This solid money is different from liquid money. The banks create what might be called longer-term solid money, money which gets entrenched in physical assets, houses, cars, businesses, roads etc. While in the American system, the Federal Reserve creates and regulates what might be deemed liquid money. This is short-term transaction money, it allows you to go buy milk, gasoline, or lets the boys on Wall Street trade stocks and bonds. It is the money by which the economy transacts on a daily basis. In order to profit from money, banks try and keep as little liquid money on hand as possible. Regulations have them keep anywhere from as little as 3% to 10%. The real trick of banking is getting all customers to believe at any given time, they can go into the bank and demand all the money they have deposited. However, as we know from history and "It's a Wonderful Life," if everyone shows up to a bank at once demanding their money, this is known as a run and the bank collapses.

This is one reason the Fed was created. There can be runs not just on deposits in banks, but on whole financial markets. These are better known as "panics." Previous to the creation of the Fed in 1913, Wall Street, and particularly John Pierpoint Morgan, would in times of panic put together liquidity, a pile of cash from various sources, providing it to those in need, though at the heavy cost of fire sale deals. After a particularly nasty panic in 1907, Morgan went to the government and said the economy had grown too large, he could no longer do it, thus a few years later the Fed was born.

The number one job of the Fed is to keep up the illusion that banks can provide all money on demand, which of course is never true. Even the name, the Federal Reserve System, gives the illusion all the money is there. Of course, it helps if you, as we did, give the Fed the power to create money in order to flood the system during times of panic. Again this is an important distinction in the money creation process of the banks, who create what might be termed longer term solid money, while the Fed creates liquid, transaction money.

The Fed and the banks are the money creators in our system. The most important question is how much money to create? You want to create enough money to keep the economy growing, while not creating too much that you create inflation. Inflation is the scourge of banks, because it devalues the solid illiquid money they have locked up in loans or investments.

Over the past three decades, the great criminal abomination that occurred, causing the current money crisis we find ourselves, is that so-called financial innovations made long-term money increasingly unstable. This was done by making what should have been solid money more liquid using such things as securitization, thereby increasing their ability to leverage their money creation process. The Fed was instrumental in providing the necessary increase in liquidity with low interest rates, and in the last few years since the 2008 Panic, using mechanisms such as ⊠uantitative Easing, the buying of various bonds such as the new mortgage securities thus turning them into cash. All this greatly distorting an already distorted money system.

So, there are a couple main problems here. Basically the stable money supply has become ever more liquid, meaning it can all disappear that much more quickly, as liquid money is by its very na-

ture transitory. In addition, by making bank money ever more liquid, they have taken the brakes off the money creation editing
process, allowing the creation of a lot of bad money. One way or
other this bad money is going to be destroyed. The greatest problem is that a good deal of debt, the supposedly longer term solid
money, is no good. It should have never been created. Much of it
was created fraudulently. As long as it exists, it will cause instability in the money system and be a hindrance to the real physical
economy.

* * *

"The Federal Reserve System was the crucial anomaly at the
very core of representative democracy, an uncomfortable contradiction with the civic mythology of self-government. Yet the
American system accepted the inconsistency. The community of
elected politicians acquiesced to its power. The private economy
responded to its direction. Private capital depended it on it for
protection. The governors of the Federal Reserve decided the
largest questions of political economy, including who shall pros-
per and who shall fail, yet their role remained opaque and mys-
terious. The Federal Reserve was shielded from scrutiny partly
by its own official secrecy, but also by the curious ignorance of
the American public." —William Greider, *Secrets of the Temple*

All money is a political construct, thus it has an element of
power. The real power in any money system is located with its creation. The constitution gives the Congress the ability to create
money, giving it the "power to coin Money, regulate the Value
thereof." Of course "coin" is an anachronism in an era of paper, and
even more so in the era of electronic money, but the Congress still
has the sole constitutional right to create money. However, a century ago, the Congress basically ceded its power to the Fed and the
banks.

The Fed simply says there is money, and there is money, sort of like Yahweh creating the heavens and earth, but faster. While the banks, maybe with even a better trick, create money from money— that is from debt. The first thing people think when they begin to understand how money is created is money should never be a hindrance to economic activity, which is only a half-truth. But the other important aspect of money is what it values, for it has no value outside the political economic system it represents.

One of the most important ways money is valued is through an accurate accounting of what's happening in the economy, and one of the best ways to insure some accuracy in that process is by dividing the money system into various components. For example, the 1930s New Deal financial regulatory system divided the money system. It kept commercial banking away from investment banking, and it used healthy Savings and Loans to further segregate housing money. Another example of this is the ability for local, state, and federal governments to issue their own bonds. These systems all use the same dollar, but the dollars in each system are separated, allowing for better accounting, better valuing, and putting a governor on how much money can be created in any given segment.

The valuing of money is the second step, money creation is the first. How much money is created certainly has an impact on its value. Relying exclusively on any given commodity, say gold, automatically limits money creation. It also gives that power to those who hold gold, which is why Keynes called gold an anti-democratic monetary standard. But allowing monopoly-creation powers to the US Federal Reserve and the banking system is also undemocratic.

There's no reason the US government needs to go to the Fed to create money, or to specific banks called "primary dealers" for debt issuance, or even create bonds for that matter. This is simply a way for private capital to both gain and game a completely unjustified profit off government activities, and in the case of funding with bonds, put an increasingly undemocratic check on public activities. There's no reason the government can't simply do its own finance, for example on large capital expenditures, or with internal activities simply account swaps of money, without allowing private capital to take what is nothing more than a vig. The same could be said to be true for state and local governments, where for many of their activities it would make perfectly good sense to simply operate as their own banks.

Such reforms would necessitate new and rigorous accounting, and in the end, the final audit in a system of self-government is done by the citizenry. Thus, any money reform can only be accomplished with a significant reform of politics and government.

* * *

"Monetary theory when all is said and done, is little more than a vast elaboration of the truth that 'it all comes out in the wash.'"
—John Maynard Keynes, *A Treatise on Money*

Over the last forty-years, money was untethered from any objective value and became another product to trade. Money became, in many respects, simply another trade in the entirety of a financialized economy. A simple definition of financialization is to indebt and "to make trade-able." However, a monetary system, and even more so an economy, that is underwater in debt and simultaneously entirely trade-able, is prone to instability and catastrophic volatility. Unless you're purely a speculator, instability is the exact opposite of what you want from a sound money system.

Keynes provided the very helpful notion that in part, money is valued through its constant interaction with the rest of the economy. Money gains value from an economy's wealth, debt, and prices. Again, for this exercise, it's not necessary to go into detail on Keynes' definitions, for as he remarks in *A Treatise,*

"The fundamental equations...are in themselves no more than identities, and therefore not intrinsically superior to other identities which have been propounded connecting monetary factors."

Phew, what trouble such honesty could cause our economic priesthood today! However, the point to be made is, at all times, money constantly interacts with the whole financial system and economy to establish value. When an economy becomes completely financialized, that is trade-able, and money is removed from all fixed standards, you allow traders to gain too strong a hand in valuing money, which increases volatility.

A system in which everything is trade-able, demands a greater volume of money to keep things liquid, literally becoming addicted to greater liquidity. What helped along the great elite financial panic in the fall of 2008 was a fall in liquidity, instigating a fall in inflated prices. Suddenly with no excess cash to keep inflated asset prices afloat, the entire system began a major contraction, racing to reach more realistic levels in a system that was not so trade-able.

Since then, the Fed, other central banks, and governments stepped-in to boost liquidity, flooding markets with dollars, euros, etc., trying to contain a continuing deflation in prices, brought about by bad debt, that is bad money. A global monetary system that is hyper-trade-able and currency value that is derived to a great extent from trading, volatility combined with what Keynes termed "sympathetic movement" creates great instability. What we need to begin to do is re-tether money. We need to make it less trade-able.

* * *

How money is defined and how it is created are essential questions for the architecture of power and the stability of any system of political economy. Outside a brief period in the 1930s, when the issue of the gold standard and the question of the government's role in creating debt popped into political debate, the money question in the United States was settled with the defeat of the Populists in the 1890s and the establishment of the Fed in 1913.

The Populists were a broad coalition comprising many elements across the late 19th century American landscape, but the majority were small and mid-size farm owners, joined by workers and the small businesses reliant on the established farming system. The Populists rose up out of the great deflationary period transpiring from the end of the Civil War until the 1890s. Deflation, a complex phenomenon caused by both money policy and technology, specifically the railroads, impacted the small American farms of the era with continually decreasing crop prices. Farmers would borrow at the beginning of the year to gain the seed and other materials needed to plant and grow, then pay back at harvest. However, if you are borrowing based on prices from last year and the next year's prices are less, you soon end up in an ever-increasing spiral of debt.

Organizing together in the Farmers Alliance, the farmers figured out a money system based on the gold standard was combining with other forces such as the new railroads to create ever falling prices and ever increasing debt, destroying both the farmers' independence and their lives. The Farmers Alliance developed a completely practical and ingenious system for allowing democratic definition, creation, and control of money. Instead of money being simply based on gold, and its creation controlled by the burgeoning industry of finance—Wall Street and the banks—the Populists devised a self-government "sub-treasury system," allowing them to directly gain credit based on the previous and coming fall harvest, that is their crops.

The idea was as practical as it was simple. Sub-treasuries would be set up in large counties across the country. Into these treasuries farmers could deposit grains, from which they could then draw money and credit provided directly by the government. Instead of gold being the only money standard, the Farmers Alliance devised a system in which the farmers themselves could create money, just like a bank, based on their crops. Not only were they basing money on very concrete and useful commodities, such as corn and cotton, which, unlike gold has real utility, they were in effect making each farmer a banker. Each farmer could create money.

The Populists lost. Over the next two decades, the banks and Wall Street gained control over the creation and definition of money, a control sealed by the creation of the Federal Reserve in 1913. The loss of any ability to control money doomed the small farm in America. Every year for over a century, there are fewer small farms. Today, they are close to extinction. There was absolutely nothing deterministic about the death of the small farms. America could have just as easily industrialized, keeping 10 or 20% of the population as small farmers, instead today we have less than 1%. It was and is purely an issue of power, and power in agriculture, finance, and most every other aspect of American political economy has done one thing over the course of the last century, become ever more centralized.

The idea of tying the value of money to useful commodities and physical production was not lost with the Populists. In his 1930 *Treatise on Money*, none other than John Maynard Keynes would promote what he called an international Tabular Standard for money—"representative money"—based on over 60 commodities, including cotton, pork, potash, copper, coal, and the basic components of modern industrial society. Instead, after WWII a new gold standard was instituted.

Without a democratic money system, there will never be much democracy. If we are going to revive and evolve democracy in this country, we need to rethink the money system. Keynes himself well understood the political implications of money and how it was controlled, writing in his 1930 *Treatise*,

"Thus the gold standard is...part of the apparatus of Conservatism. ...gold, originally stationed in heaven with his consort silver, as Sun and Moon, having first doffed his sacred attributes and come to earth as an autocrat, may next descend to the sober status of a constitutional king with a cabinet of banks; and it may never be necessary to proclaim a Republic. But this is not yet—the evolution may be quite otherwise. The friends of gold will to have be extremely wise and moderate if they are to avoid a Revolution."

Gold was dethroned in the early 70s, though there are certainly many old courtiers clamoring for its restoration. But, at this point our money system has an even greater problem. With an unchecked Fed, Wall Street, and ever-increasing concentration of banking power in several corporations, we have the most autocratic money system in our republic's history.

Breaking up the big banks is the first step in democratizing our money system, simultaneously destroying a lot of the bad money that was created in the last several decades. A politics of default can be initiated. You hold mortgages or securities on underwater mortgages, sorry you lose, the mortgages need to be written down to the value of the house. You hold bonds on streets to ex-urbs, you lose. You hold bonds on inefficient electric utilities, you're going to lose some, etc. The second part of the politics of default is determining what investments are good; schools—yes, mass transit—yes, community redesign infrastructure—yes.

Money can be used for two things, investment or consumption. The latter of course is easier to define, as it simply means the purchasing of goods and services to consume. While investment, in theory, uses money to create future wealth for utilization, this has become a much more complex affair over the last few decades.

One way Keynes points to value money is by tying its creation to savings. He writes,

"According to my own definition "sound credit conditions" would, of course, be those in which the market-rate of interest was equal to the natural-rate, and both the value and the cost of new investment were equal to the volume of current savings."

Over the last several decades in America, we've seen a complete untying of the correlation between investment and savings. This can be re-instituted.

The savings rate has dropped through the floor, while investment, and here I mean the entire financial system, has blown through the roof. Now there are plenty of reasons for how this came about, but this fundamental disconnect, growing with the fundamental changes in the American economy has led to an incredibly unstable global monetary system.

The financial innovations of the last three decades can be rescinded. Most importantly, the banks and the Fed need to lose their monopoly on money creation. It is time to take away the majority of the decision making processes on the economy from the bankers and spread it across the economy—Democratize It!

IV. THE POLITICAL ECONOMY OF ENERGY

1. OIL

We watched the financial system help bring down the economy, but the fact is all finance remains a sideshow to what is really the main event of modern life—energy. The harnessing of fossil fuels pretty much defines what we call modern. No nation on the planet is more proliferate in its use of energy than the United States, thus American life for the past hundred years has been equated with modernity. The most important element for American modernism is oil, or more accurately, cheap oil, and this is becoming increasingly problematic.

America first became aware of our oil dependence back in the 70s, but did little about it except expand our military in an attempt to secure remaining global resources, overwhelming located around the Persian Gulf. The simple accounting fact is the finding of new global oil sources topped-out in the mid-1960s and has pretty much steadily sloped down every year since. Over the last decade, it's been a struggle for the oil industry to even keep discoveries equal to existing use.

Most recently, the United States largest oil program was the occupation of Iraq, and we will not be disentangled from Iraq until we solve our oil addiction. Stuart Staniford of The Oil Drum wrote an interesting piece about the redeveloping of Iraq's oil industry. The Iraqis claim they can eventually pump 12 million barrels a day. This is very hard to believe for many, many reasons. It would mean the Iraqis increasing total global production by over 10%. But, let's say they're right. It would be good news for the world only in the sense Staniford's piece points out, it gives the world more time to transition away from oil. However, there is no sign of this transition anywhere, particularly in the US, and of course China, India and others are going full bore in building their own oil dependence—call it modernity.

Thinking about energy gives a whole new meaning to the term post-modern. Every idea about future economic health needs to be tied to a transition away from oil. The good ideas don't for the most part include present bio-fuels, particularly the turning of foodstuffs into transportation fuels. The American ethanol program is immoral, plain and simple, but there are problems with many bio-fuels.

Energy remains the foundation of any discussion about our economic future. One easy thing to understand, burning isn't a solution. For America, it means conservation and efficiency foremost, our waste being of such horrendous magnitude there's plenty to gain. The other is the sun and after many years of procrastinating, we seem finally to be getting serious about it. And that's much better news that any increase in Iraq oil production.

* * *

The Financial Times published a piece on BP dumping much of their alternative energy activity. As someone who has followed and been in the energy world far too long, it's not surprising in the least. BP made a big PR hullabaloo back in the 1990s claiming they had literally seen the energy light and our future was "Beyond Petroleum." I pointed out at the time, and since, that BP spent much more money advertising they were "Beyond Petroleum" than actually doing anything. I concluded the whole thing was more PR than reality when a decade ago I attended a dinner with the head of BP Solar, a Scotsman. I said they had to move the business model of solar from low volume–high margin to high volume–low margin, following the lead of the semi-conductor industry. He looked at me and said, "Well laddie, its not about how cheap we can make it. It's about how much we can make you pay." Welcome to the oil industry.

Now, there is no greater imperative for the future of the United States and the entire world than to move beyond petroleum. One can make a list of the reasons why—environmental, economic, or the one that moves me most personally, I don't think we should be killing people and spending trillions of dollars on weapons of destruction so that we can encase our obese bodies in two tons of steel and rubber, calling it freedom. Remember, BP started out a hundred years ago as the Anglo-Persian Oil Company, when Mr. D'Arcy finally hit pay dirt in what is now Iran. And Americans once again become so concerned about the Iran, we should remember, it was when the democratically elected parliament of Iran nationalized the oil industry that Prime Minister Mossaddeq was overthrown by an American coup d'etat. The Shah was installed, and the rest as they say is history.

There's a great lesson concerning BP and alternative energy. Change will not come though giant entrenched institutions. Change will come by forcing them to loosen their power, or simply by breaking them up. Giant entrenched institutions are giant bureaucracies that focus on preserving the status quo. This is their mission, not change. Yet, the political fight in America today, such that it is, is all about grabbing for the levers of centralized power, increasingly futile attempts to change giant entrenched institutions. Healthcare, energy, the financial system, you name it. Leave it intact, put someone new at the top, and everything will be different, so we are told.

Blood and oil have mixed well together for a very long time. We need to tax oil big time. Let's start by bringing the price to $5 a gallon. "Well you can't do that! We're in a recession!" Yes, that's exactly right and there's no way we're going to bring back the oil-drenched economy of the past century. Bringing the price of oil up will necessitate a reform and restructuring of the American economy requiring everyone to participate, not a continuation of the awful empty pantomime carried out in the boardrooms of the mega-corporations or in our co-opted halls of power in Washington DC.

* * *

It is not coincidental that you can trace the beginning of the transformation of the American economy from one based on physical production to a rentier racket, at approximately the time domestic American oil production peaked in 1970, followed closely by the oil shocks of the 1970s. The American economy was irrevocably changed.

Cheap oil, not money, be it the dollar, yuan, yen or euro, is the foundation of modern life. The most astounding fact of recent American life is how for three decades, we've done everything we can to avoid the issue, increasingly harming the American economy and the entire global economy. For years, I've been using the simple fact if three-quarters of the Chinese used oil on the same per capita basis as Americans, and Americans continued doing the same, there would be no oil for anyone else on the planet—no one! The faster China grows using its current model, the faster we get to this point.

It is for this exact reason that Chinese per capita economic growth rate will not be able to continue its pace. Call it the Oil Yoke. As soon as global economic growth reaches a certain rate, the price of oil is going to choke it right back down. This gives truth to the biggest lie of corporate globalization—that the world can live like Americans do. Well, not even Americans can live like Americans anymore. But that's okay, we can live better. In the short-run, this certainly doesn't help the Chinese, whose centrally controlled economy went full force in building a cheap oil infrastructure, only to belatedly find out cheap oil doesn't exist anymore.

When we talk about reform, whether it's financial, political, or industrial, it all starts at one place, with energy. America has reached peak-energy consumption, and no amount of money the Fed pumps into the system is going to change that. We have both the necessity and tremendous opportunity to restructure the American economy based on renewable energy sources and even more imperative, design it to use a lot less energy than we use today. We have both the knowledge and capability, but we lack the will. Having reached peak energy consumption, creating an economy based on renewables and design efficiency will not be adding new wealth, but distributing existing wealth, and that is going to require hardheaded political and financial reform. We could do a lot worse than to start by tying money to energy.

* * *

The International Energy Agency announced recently that the world is going to become increasingly reliant on OPEC for oil, more accurately the Persian Gulf, as other members of OPEC will soon enough be formerly petroleum exporting countries. According to the Wall Street Journal,

> "The global dependency on the members of the Organization of Petroleum Exporting Countries for oil will rise in the next five to 10 years as production by non-OPEC nations declines, the chief of the International Energy Agency said Friday."

> "We have seen an increase in non-OPEC supplies. But in the mid-term, non-OPEC production will decline," Nobuo Tanaka, the agency's executive director, told reporters on the sidelines of a conference. "So, dependency on OPEC oil will increase."

> OPEC's 12 members, who include Saudi Arabia, the United Arab Emirates and Kuwait, account for about 40% of the global oil (production)."

I guess a trend that's been going on for over three decades now is news. Here are some better numbers, not that numbers have any relation to economic reality these days. The countries around the Persian Gulf have 60% of known global oil reserves, while the EU, the US, China and Japan, who conveniently enough account for 60% of the world's economy, have only 9% of the world's remaining oil reserves. If you cut the US out of that equation it would drop to 3%.

The entire corporate globalization experiment of the past few decades is built on the premise of cheap oil. The entire global oil market, increasingly unable to provide cheap oil, is built on the American military, and the American military is built on debt, each year becoming ever more unsustainable. Now, we could go to the EU, China, and Japan and say you guys need to start kicking-in to pay for our military service, but I doubt that would go over well with anyone. First, no one's going to give money without a corresponding increase in say. Or we can begin to realize that the entire corporate globalization experiment, premised on cheap oil, is at best problematic and more accurately a failure. We as a planet need to begin creating a non-oil based economy, that is, we need to truly become post-modern. But when you have an economy, politics, and culture completely addicted to oil, that's difficult. Getting off oil is Job-1 for any sustained economic revival, meaning a complete redesign of our economic infrastructure.

2. FOSSIL FUEL CULTURE

Gore Vidal looks at the signing of the National Security Act of 1947 by the hapless Harry Truman—why, oh why America, do you still insist on electing anyone president?—as the official beginning of the National Security State. It was the first time after a war the United States did not shrink our military, but instead institutionalized a war-time budget. Over six decades this became the single greatest contributor to America's perpetual growing debt, and maybe more importantly, it led the gross processes of corruption and degradation that have come to defile and define American politics.

In The Oil Kings, author Andrew Scott Cooper, using recently declassified American government communications, shows how simply abhorrent, obscene, and massively incompetent the National Security State is. Telling the sad story of America's growing obsession from 1968 to 1978 with the Persian Gulf, and its reservoirs of remaining global oil, Cooper paints a tragic-comedy picture of the pathetic and despicable Mistah Nixon and his blood lust twin Henry Kissinger stumbling into the Persian Gulf with little knowledge of oil or its importance to the economy. The Tweedledee and Tweedledum of American Cold War incompetence prop-up the Eisenhower era National Security State CIA installed Shahanshah of Iran to be the bulwark of the south, in their paranoid megalomaniac game against the Red Menace, at the time an increasingly faltering Soviet Union.

Mr. Nixon and Mr. Kissinger work with the "Hand of God on Earth" to cobble together OPEC, so that oil prices can stay firm, while the Shah pumps more oil to buy more American military products. In fact, the ignorant Mr. Nixon tells the Shah, he can raise oil prices specifically to buy more military goods, without a clue to the importance of cheap oil to the oil dependent US economy. Unbeknownst to Mr. Nixon and the entire American establishment, US oil production peaks in 1970, thus three years later, when OPEC led by America's Persian Emperor ally, triples the price of oil, the global economy is shocked and falls to its knees for the rest of the 1970s, only to be relieved temporarily by America's newer ally in the Gulf, with greater oil reserves than His Royal Majesty of Iran, the House of Saud.

While *The Oil Kings* details the important story of America's incompetent oil policy, it more importantly reveals acute aspects of corruption and unaccountable power that are the American National Security State, showing that just like in banking and finance, the machinations of National Security State are beyond our politics. Where the corruption of banking and finance is upheld by some nebulous notion marketed as capitalism, the National Security State is placed beyond politics with an even more nebulous and nefarious notion of patriotism.

In fact, the National Security State wrote much of the playbook for corruption in DC, while everyone else played catch-up. Mr. Cooper writes of retired Colonel Richard Hallock's 1975 report to then Defense Secretary Schlesinger:

"The US government's policy of foreign military sales pricing "is not correct or consistent and often not honest...the credibility problem is deeper than the absolute costs; and it is heightened by the fact that nearly every case questioned by the (government of Iran) shows that there were overcharges with abuses. The amount of money that Iran is spending with the US together with the lack of leadership and discipline...has greatly increased the corruption in the FMS (foreign military sales) system in the Services." Hallock warned of "marriages of interest between the Services and major contractors for conducting of business in Iran which is not authorized by either the Secretary of Defense or (the government of Iran)—projects born of deception and lies greased by influence and payoffs."

"An example of such corruption was the 1972 Gruman deal cooked up by Nelson Rockefeller and Kissinger. It had finally drawn the scrutiny of Congressional investigators and led to embarrassment for the Pentagon. The probe uncovered evidence that Gruman had agreed to pay "commissions" to Iranian middleman in the amount of $20 million over five years starting in 1972. "It was normal practice," claimed Gruman's president, John Bierworth. Members of Congress demanded to know why Gruman was forking out millions in kickbacks at a time when the company was taking taxpayer dollars in the form of a loan extended by the Pentagon for it to stay in business—and whether this deal was connected to a second $200 million loan offered by Bank Melli of Iran, the bank that enjoyed close commercial ties with David Rockefeller."

A year later, the Senate would release a report saying "US arms sales to Iran were 'out of control' and that Iran couldn't go to war 'without US support on a day to day basis' The report warned that tens of thousands of Americans living in Iran were potential hostages if relations between Washington and Tehran ever broke down." And the rest as they say is history. America's great ally in the Gulf, the "King of Kings," consistently spending over a third of his government's revenues on military expenditures, was unceremoniously dumped by the people of Iran in 1979, along with it tumbled America's fortress on the Gulf. Iran remains a pariah in the eyes of America's institutions for three decades and counting. Bureaucracies have long memories.

Since then, the National Security State, its corruption and incompetence, have only grown in size. The American economy remains existentially dependent on cheap oil and military spending gobbles up over a trillion dollars a year. There are no more Congressional hearings on the gross corruption and blood stained graft as members of both parties, from all sides of America's infinitesimal political spectrum are owned by what Mr. Eisenhower labeled the Military Industrial Complex. Even those great 60s raised politicians from the Newt and Dick Cheney to Mr. Bill, who did everything they could to run from the National Security State service in their youth, all became its great proponents in their rise to the top.

There will be no reform of American politics and there will be no revitalization of the American economy without ending the National Security State and America's oil addiction.

* * *

The IEA published a study stating global fossil fuel subsidies amount to almost $600 billion a year. I guarantee that's vastly, vastly under counted, but it's an improvement over ten years ago when I was working in the energy world. At that time, there was one study from the late 1990s, from the IMF or World Bank, estimating fossil fuel subsidies around $200 billion. It was pretty much the only study, as subsidies for oil are considered no such thing by industrial economics, just part of the natural order.

At this point, the renewable energy industry, who I was working with, was dead in the water. Their existence completely dependent on subsidies, and of course, it being the pinnacle of America's Friedmanite, Randian, Greenspanian, free marketeer era, the renewable industry spent most of it's time trying to convince the few government officials who would listen that the renewable industry would eventually strive in the "free-market," despite the fact after over a century, oil and other fossil fuels remained fully subsidized. To broach the topic of the existence of fossil fuel subsidies in established energy circles was to be considered absurd. That is real power.

Much of our economic thinking today is simply a rationalizing of the existing power of our mega-corporations, centralized government, and just as importantly, though far less understood, entrenched technologies. Lawrence Goodwyn made an excellent point in the The Populist Moment:

"A far more permanent and thus far more desirable solution to the task of achieving domestic tranquility is cultural—the creation of mass modes of thought that literally make the need for major additional social changes difficult for the mass of the population to imagine. When and if achieved, these conforming modes of thought and conduct constitute the new culture itself. The ultimate victory is nailed into place, therefore, only when the population has been persuaded to define all conceivable political activity within the limits of existing custom. Such a society can genuinely be described as "stable." Thenceforth, protest will pose no ultimate threat because the protesters will necessarily conceive of their options as being so limited that even should they be successful, the resulting "reforms" will not alter significantly the inherited modes of power and privilege."

This is power's greatest trick, and by no means necessarily illegitimate, in fact essential for any sort of continuous power structure. Putting aside the question of legitimacy, there comes a time when many of the "conforming modes of thought and conduct" constituting the culture of power are no longer viable. The contradictions between ruling cultural doctrine and reality become not simply unsustainable, but in fact detrimental. For our society, if present unaccounted subsidies for oil, for example, were actually accounted, it would be obviously apparent they are both unsustainable and detrimental.

Culture can warp reality for awhile, but not endlessly. Counter to the propaganda of our meeska-mouska-free marketeers, subsidies can be perfectly fine. You do however need to account for them. Subsidies can be ways in which political economy influences the society's direction, thus you need a healthy politics for this to function well. Today, the culture created by centralized corporate and government power is not only unaccountable, but failing spectacularly. We need to fix our markets and our government, starting with some honest accounting.

* * *

"There it is, take it." —William Mulholland on the first water coursing the Los Angeles Aqueduct

The history of the Los Angeles Department of Water and Power (DWP) is one of the great stories of US history, offering great lessons on many things, maybe most importantly on reform. The DWP was created over a hundred years ago to bring water to Los Angeles. Without taking water from elsewhere in the state, Los Angeles would have remained a dusty little desert byway. It was started by a man with vision, William Mulholland. His first vision was to take the water that drained from the Eastern Sierras into the Owens Valley and pipe it a couple hundred miles south to Los Angeles. There were two great obstacles. The first was the building of the aqueduct, including pumping it over some mountains. The second was relieving the current Owens Valley water users of their rights, initiating one of the most under reported wars in American history, led by Mr. Mulholland and the DWP against the farmers of the Owens Valley. Today, it's always a hoot to head up to the northern Owens valley, over 300 miles from downtown LA, and run into vast fenced areas marked, "No Trespassing! Property of LADWP."

Ten or so years later, the DWP would add electricity to its mix, and grow to become one of the most powerful public agencies in the country. Today, the DWP is the great heart for the vast empire which is Los Angeles. Now, LA takes water from the Eastern and Western Sierras, and from the Colorado River too. The majority of its electricity comes from a number of coal plants in Nevada, Utah, and Arizona, while the Department itself evolved into one massive byzantine bureaucracy, fighting off all change and crushing all personalities who attempt reform.

The Los Angeles Times recently published two good stories on the DWP and the tragic state of California politics. In the first, two appointees of LA's hapless Mayor Antonio Villaraigosa bicker so much the DWP hires...wait for it...a psychologist, to try to smooth things over. Old Mulholland must be violently spinning in his grave! For almost twenty years, I've watched the DWP chew up and spit out so-called reformers. At one point I even sat in a couple meetings with a self-proclaimed reformer on the top floor in the chairman's office. He left no impact. And just to show who is in charge, in the second article, the DWP bureaucracy announces forget switching to renewables, coal works just fine.

Los Angeles should be leading the world in solar energy production. When you fly into LAX you should pass over an ocean of roofs making energy. But ask anyone in the solar industry and LA is a dead zone, and that's because of the DWP. The DWP not only controls LA's water and electricity, but they also give to the city itself a share of the revenue, over 6% of its budget, thus making the city itself an ally of the status quo. The DWP represents the problem of entrenched interests, and they can be public or private, in any system in need of change. In this particular case of a powerful public agency, the bureaucracy fights off as a threat all attempts at change.

The DWP is just another example of entrenched power and interests that dominate this country at this point. The Department's history represents a natural order of politics, where a vibrant new vision creates, gradually institutionalizes, and then eventually grows stagnant, to the point where vitality is considered a threat. When things reach such a level, there's no hope of changing the institution itself, instead power must be broken-up, it needs to be distributed, so change can take place. There is no middle ground, no splitting the difference when things have reached such a point. Reform is simply those losing power and those gaining.

3. TRANSPORTATION

The county of Los Angeles has ten million people, the most populous in the nation. LA developed with the automobile. Much of the time, it is a transportation nightmare, both so massively inefficient and plain inhuman it boggles the mind. Yet the automobile, barely a century old, remains the ultimate symbol of freedom for modern America. At this point, reality couldn't be further from the truth. *The Los Angeles Times* published a good piece on LA transportation and the price of freedom:

> "Los Angeles marked Transportation Freedom Day last week. What's that? It's the day when the typical median-income family has earned enough money to cover transportation costs for the entire year.

> "Your basic middle-class L.A. household spends about $8,600 a year on gas, insurance, parking and vehicle maintenance, according to the California Public Interest Research Group, a watchdog organization.

"That compares with about $8,000 for the average U.S. family and represents more than 20% of most people's annual expenditures."

Ten weeks of work a year just to pay the oil, automobile, and insurance industries—freedom indeed! I did a rough calculation, way good enough for energy numbers, an industry whose numbers make Wall Street's accounting look rigorous. At $3 a gallon, the County of LA sends fifteen billion dollars a year straight out of the local economy simply for the cost of oil. Call it an oil industry tax.

In fits and pieces, LA has attempted to do public transit, but the only thing worse than sitting in a car in the middle of LA traffic is sitting on a bus. *The Los Angeles Times'* David Lazarus writes,

"My car was in the shop last week, and I rode public transit around town. I don't mind going by bus or rail—it's a nice change from playing road warrior. In fact, I'd willingly ride public transportation every day if the system were more user-friendly.

"But it's not. And it's almost as if the dozens of entities that constitute the region's public-transit network are conspiring to make the system as unwelcoming as possible."

Now this is an important point, government has actively subsidized automobile usage in this country for a century. Los Angeles County has 88 local municipal governments to coordinate, making any reasonable transit plan a challenge. But an important question is instead of what would traditionally be the solution of placing power into some over-all central authority, how can we get these entities working together in some sort of distributed networked system? Doing so would be a fundamental element in reforming and evolving self-government for the 21st century. Open architecture, open standards and cooperative integration, three elements of the still young Internet era can be important components in evolving LA transit.

* * *

File under if you live long enough, one of the most optimistic trends for America in the last several decades,

> "Selling cars to young adults under 30 is proving to be a real challenge for automakers. Unlike their elders, Generation Yers own fewer cars and don't drive much. They're likely to see autos as a source of pollution, not as a sex or status symbol."

> "They're more apt to ride mass transit to work and use car sharing services—pioneered by Zipcar—for longer trips. And car sharing choices are expanding, with car rental firms moving into the market, making it convenient for young folks to rent with hourly rates and easy insurance. Connect by Hertz, for example, is rolling out its car sharing services in the New York metropolitan area, with plans to eventually expand them to around 40 college campuses nationwide.

> "Moreover, in survey after survey, Gen Yers say that they believe cars are damaging to the environment. Even hybrid electric vehicles don't seem to be changing young consumers' attitudes much."

What's most interesting is the politics of cars has yet to make it onto any political platform in America, except those of your real crackpots. Phew, nothing defined 20th century America more than the automobile. Across the board—political economy, culture, and the politics of technology—changing the automobile infrastructure is talking about revolution.

* * *

"A large number of suburban working poor may now be stranded: A survey of riders in April 2008 found that 65% of them do not have access to a car. In a survey last month, 3 out of 4 said they may lose their jobs when the buses stopped rolling."

Can you imagine people in the US not having a car, and not having a car living in a suburban area? Why don't they have a car? They can't afford it. Why, isn't a car an essential part of the last half of the 20th century American Dream? The article further states,

"Since 1995, public transportation use is up 31%, more than twice the U.S. population growth rate, according to the American Public Transportation Assn., the nonprofit that represents the nation's commuter systems. Last year, Americans took 10.2 billion public transit trips."

People didn't increase their public transit use out of environmental concern, no, solely for economic reasons. Cutting public transit is the last thing we should be doing, we should be doing just the opposite, investing more, yet,

"In a survey of 151 (public transit) member agencies released Thursday, the association found that about 9 in 10 of them reported flat or decreased local and state funding. Nearly 3 in 5 had already cut service or raised fares."

Understand, when the economy fails tens of millions of people on an essential element like transportation, it is failing grandly. So, when you see all the anger being vented, remember what really underlies it: an American economy that increasingly works for fewer and fewer people. Eldrin Bell, a black Commissioner of Clayton County put it best, "I've lived with racism, But this is a new one—it's called classism. I've never seen anything like it."

When class becomes entrenched in America that will truly be the death of the American Dream.

4. ENERGY WEALTH DISTRIBUTION

The term wealth redistribution gets bandied about mostly negatively. Much of the time, it is the fault of its proponents, who start at the ends, instead of looking at the means. For example, we have an economy that produces "X" amount, so the way to redistribute wealth is to tax a certain % of "X", and redistribute it through various government programs, call this progressive. This is all fine and well as far it goes, but the problem is it increasingly doesn't go nearly far enough, call that liberal. However, a more important way to look at wealth redistribution is to look at it from the means part of the equation, not at the end wealth, but the technology and processes creating the wealth, call this democracy.

Looking at the electricity industry, the politics of wealth redistribution is not the question of dividing up the spoils, but dividing up the process itself, for example replacing entrenched technologies with newer technologies. The architecture of the electric industry is a century old. It is based on giant centralized generation plants, pumping energy through a network of wires to hundreds of thousands of distributed households, businesses, schools etc. This system is run by government bestowed monopolies, who control both the technology and the politics of electricity. If anyone wanted to see how government regulators are eventually captured by the regulated, all they need do is look at the utilities.

Not only is the technology entrenched and protected by law, but so too finance. Utilities are forever issuing more debt, which is considered some of the best and hardest money. Energy is about as hard a money you can get these days. To simply tax or regulate the profits, considered traditional wealth redistribution, is to miss the point. In the 21st century, wealth redistribution lies in changing the electricity system architecture, taking the wealth from central- ized generation, massive transmission systems, and utility debt holders, and instead, transferring it to distributed generation, such as solar on your roof and efficiency in your home, micro-grid net- works comprised of aggregated distributed generators, much greater use of information technologies, and new financing.

The price of solar technology has fallen tremendously in the last few years due finally, after fifty-years, to some real investment in the last decade. The head of the massive energy conglomerate NGR states,

> "We will be in a situation where within two years the price of delivered power from solar installations will be able to undercut the retail price of grid power in roughly 20 states," Crane said. "Many of these high-price retail states are in our core regions. This low-cost solar power, installed in ever-increasing volumes on a distributed and semi-distributed basis in a way that obvi- ates the need for a lot of very long high-voltage transmission lines, has a potential to revolutionize the hub-and-spoke power system which currently makes up the American power indus- try."

Mr. Crane will find price is not the only determining factor in utility economics. Nonetheless, we are on the cusp of being able to redistribute fundamental modern wealth in this country at a tremendous level, yet, it must be understood, this is not creating wealth beyond what there is now, but transferring existing energy wealth into other forms, including from existing technology, debt, massive utility corporations, and representative government regulatory structures. These will all be replaced by other technologies, new utility structures, new finance, and new democratic government systems. This is the politics of wealth redistribution—this is reform politics of 21st century America.

* * *

The transistor and the photo-voltaic cell were invented at roughly the same time. However, the amount of money spent developing the transistor and the microchip exponentially dwarfs the amount spent on developing the solar cell and all other forms of renewable energy combined. There are important reasons for this and they're essential to understanding the political economy of technology.

First, energy from fossil fuels in the early 1950s was relatively cheap, subsidized, and the costs of its environmental impact socialized. Nuclear fission, the military-industrial complex's new energy technology became the designated energy of the future and devoured almost all energy development dollars.

Secondly, energy was monopoly controlled. In the case of electricity, the reform of the electric industry in the 1930s created a system controlled by state sanctioned public and private monopolies. While the oil industry's conglomerates are not officially state sanctioned, they are nonetheless monopolistic. Technologies create their own infrastructures, companies, bureaucracies, and even elected officials, whose most important job becomes protecting the established technology. This creates a problem, as much political as it is economic or technological, in replacing entrenched technologies. From an energy perspective, the swapping-out of existing fossil energy sources with renewable sources creates no new net societal wealth, except for in areas of environmental restitution. It is a process of wealth redistribution, taking wealth from established power and transferring it to new or older processes. In most cases, the established power is intimately entwined with the state. Understanding this in all its facets gives you a better understanding of the political economy of energy.

* * *

The recent UAW deal that saved GM included, a cutting of a third of their jobs, the offshoring of some manufacturing facilities by their government, and the cutting in half of wages for new hires.

According to *The Wall Street Journal,*

"To date, 16,000 to 18,000 people have participated in more than five dozen pilot tests involving smart meters and experimental rate plans, according to Ahmad Faruqui, a consultant with the Brattle Group who has helped utilities develop some of the programs. He says that while it is sometimes disheartening to see utility executives ignore their own findings, he understands the desire to move slowly until people become comfortable with smart-meter technology."

That's a pretty small number, but it's a start. The biggest problem of course is the utilities, who having run the system pretty much the same way for almost a century, don't see much need to change. The simple agreement has been the utilities provide electricity at a reasonable, and some would say a very cheap rate, thus people basically allow the utilities to run things however they want. Leading to the second problem: most electricity users pay very little attention to how they use electricity, first and foremost because it's so cheap.

Information is always cheaper than energy, and getting more information into the system will facilitate change. I am astounded in dealing with the electricity industry how it is almost universally accepted that more information about how things are run, won't prove of any value. This is still a big problem and as the article points out, the utilities don't even know what to do with the information they are receiving. Simply giving them more information isn't going to help, or will not be as helpful as it should be. Political reform needs very much to be utility reform. We need to open the system so that not just the utilities, but others, most importantly consumers, are allowed enact necessary change.

According to *The Wall Street Journal,*

> "You could have a real rebellion" if smart meters push up customers' rates, especially if utilities' other capital expenses are increasing, he says.

There are probably few industries with as much fixed capital debt as the utilities, and it seems this debt is never ending. It is an important point for the United States. We are an extremely wealthy nation, however much of our fixed capital, particularly in regards to the energy sector, is a problem. We have to change how this operates. The more debt we pile on the existing infrastructure, the more difficult that change is going to be. Unlike the developing world, where such infrastructure is limited, adding to it creates wealth. In the United States, changing this infrastructure is not creating new wealth, but transferring established wealth to new purposes. It is an extremely important distinction. Power is going to have devolve from the utilities.

Electricity users must educate themselves and be part of the change. Being a citizen in the 21st century means understanding energy.

V. THE POLITICS OF TECHNOLOGY

1. RAILROADS

The history of American railroads is first and foremost a story of the politics of technology. Yet, because we have such a limited understanding of this phenomenon, in fact we have almost zero, it disallows us from delving to the sources of many of the challenges we face. There's a new book call *Railroaded*, which from a review seems to broach some issues of the politics of technology. The reviewer writes of the author's thesis:

> "Transcontinental railroads," he asserts in *Railroaded*, "were a Gilded Age extravagance that rent holes in the political, social and environmental fabric of the nation, creating railroads as mismanaged and corrupt as they were long."

We need much more thinking about the politics of technology. For example, the modern corporate structure was birthed and made possible by industrial technology. The corporate structure is anti-democratic, combined with the power of industrial technology, the industrial corporation ran roughshod over the nascent democratic structures of America's early agrarian/merchant republic. These structures were still new and very delicate, for history offered few models and even less experience in democratic culture and republican institutions.

Unfortunately, we can't look to the leaders in technology for thinking on politics, for almost to the man, they have accepted profit as supreme value, which is why something like Facebook, can be talked about as the future, for a couple years anyway. While others, such as a former editor of Wired seek to turn technology into a new religion, be very leery brothers and sisters of those who seek to start new religions, they tend to be the lowest lot.

2. THE AUTOMOBILE

The automobile doesn't simply represent our "modern age," it is in many ways the American modern age. In the mid-1950s, one in eight jobs in the United States was tied directly to the automobile. What we came to know as the American middle-class rode to existence in the automobile. Organized labor, which provided the wage growth for middle class life, came into its own in Flint, Michigan. Across the planet, one could discern the development of any nation's economy by whether it has a domestic auto industry—Mexico yes, Tanzania no.

Yet, the automobile is even much more. It shows the power any given technology can assert on a society. Technologies create their own cultures, or as Marshall McLuhan stated a half century ago, first we shape technologies and then technologies shape us. There is no greater heresy in America today than to tell people you don't necessarily need an automobile. You might as well say there is no God. This is easily understood because the automobile has so shaped America, one has to have quite the imagination to think we can get by, and get by well, without one.

America's automobile era ended in 1970, when US oil production peaked. It was a shock to the 70s, though there was a false reprieve in the 80s and 90s, but across this time automobile culture was slowly, or with a slightly longer view of history, rather quickly collapsing. UAW membership peaked in 1979 and now is less than a third. The recent UAW deal that saved GM included, a cutting of the third of their jobs, the offshoring of some manufacturing facilities by their government, and the cutting in half of wages for new hires. The American middle class peaked in the 70s, wages stagnant for three decades now. This hollowing-out is obscured by the indebting of the majority of Americans over the past three decades.

The saving of GM means nothing, in fact just the opposite, it reveals what a long way we have to go in confronting necessary fundamental changes. Post-World War II automobile culture is not going to be saved by more fuel efficiency or better battcries. Our continued clinging to automobile culture will be detrimental to the future, just as the last three decades has been for today. We need a fundamental re-think of not only our transportation infra-structure, but our communities themselves, indeed how we define modern life. What's good for GM never has been and still isn't good for America.

3. THE NETWORKED-MICROPROCESSOR

Economics is not a science. It is a political, cultural, and social construct defining how any given society designs and runs the processes of production, distribution, and consumption of physical goods. In creating these processes, any given economic system also creates a system of worth, by which all things interacting with these processes are valued. A failing economic system can have many causes, but one characteristic they all have in common is previous value no longer holds. What was once highly valued, suddenly becomes less so, while other things once deemed of not great worth, may become increasingly more so. In order to reform a failing economic system, value must be revalued, and this is where we find ourselves today.

The failing corporate globalization model has many methods and processes that divine value, some centuries or even millenia old. However, let's focus on several that are little more than a half-century to a century and a half old, including the oil economy, the Pax Americana, and most recent, the networked-microprocessor. In many ways, the cheap oil economy precedes corporate globalization, the Pax Americana is more or less congruent, while the networked micro-processor is both its pinnacle and its downfall.

The present economic system places value on all aspects of the globe from the labor of a Chinese worker, to homes in American suburbs, farmland in Africa, and banks in Greece. As this system continues to falter, values become more volatile. We have one of two choices; to attempt and increasingly fail to maintain present values, leading to an even more inequitable system that is ever more violent, or to begin a process of reform, creating new political, cultural, and social processes of the production, distribution, and consumption of physical goods—a process of revaluing value.

There are two main means to beginning this process. The first is to raise the price of oil and the second is to initiate a process of debt destruction, that acknowledges certain values based on the system of corporate globalization can no longer be maintained, while at the same time making new investments based on the advantages and constraints of locality. Once these things are started, we can start a new process of valuing trade, not based simply on obscene profits for the few.

Maybe most importantly, the networked-microprocessor will continue to make redundant more and more aspects of industrial labor, while creating an ever new information environment, which cannot properly be valued by the present corporate globalization system, or even the older industrial economic system. It is a system that will give value with processes we have traditionally ascribed to the political as opposed to the economic. It means revaluing the citizen.

* * *

We must stop the concentration of wealth in our developing information culture. Microsoft, Amazon, Google, and most obscene yet, Facebook, are the industrial corporate structure being used to con-

centrate the wealth generated with new technologies. Paradoxically, they use new technologies, which give us the ability to create
a new democratic distributed networked order, but instead we create new concentrations of wealth. Microsoft used its control of the
operating system to ruthlessly concentrate wealth for its top brass.
Google co-opted the distributed openness of the Net's architecture,
giving it a more centralized order, while Facebook incredulously
mines the data of its users to sell to others.

What we have learned in the brief history of the networked-microprocessor is technology may have certain determinant factors,
and of course, its very adaption changes the society which preceded it, but without a politics, even the most inherently distributed technologies can be used to concentrate power. And if the
networked-microprocessor is to reach its democratic promise,
those concerned about its evolution are going to have to become
much more concerned with the evolution of the society of which it
is part. As Mr. Brandeis would well have understood, to gain political liberty we must attend not just economic and industrial liberty,
but technological liberty.

* * *

"Accelerated change invokes the gyroscopic or principles of
rigidity. Also, to high-speed change no adjustment is possible.
We become spectators only, and must escape into understanding. This may be why the conservative has an advantage in such
an age of speedy change and is frequently more radical in his
suggestions and insights than the progressive who is trying to
adjust. The practical progressive trying to make realistic adjust-
ments to change exhausts himself in minor matters and has no
energy to contemplate the overall." —Marshall McLuhan, 1960

As many of America's founders understood, there is no societal
element more fundamental for healthy self-government than a free

press. Of course, the technologies of a free press have changed radically over the republic's relatively short two-centuries history. At our republic's founding, a free press was literally that, a printing press, producing newspapers, periodicals, pamphlets and books. This was altered with the wider geographic spectrum offered fifty years later with the telegraph, then radically redefined with the birth of broadcast media. The control of radio and television by three corporations decimated the previous media landscape, concentrating the control of communications media, (the free press), to a degree unprecedented in American history. As far as the republic was concerned, there never was a Golden Age of broadcast media.

In the last few decades, mega-corporate controlled broadcast media came under attack first and briefly from cable, and secondly and still developing from the Internet. With the understanding that a free press is essential to self-government, an essential component of any reform politics will be establishment of a vital communications network, in the same manner every reform effort in American history initiated itself with the publication of a newspaper.

A reform communications network would consist of various Internet tools, such as websites, allowing the creation and dissemination of news, thought, and data pieces, created by both paid writers and with contributions from members. The sites would be networked by issue and geography, then interconnected in every way possible. The communications network would have two main goals; first, providing a narrative that challenges the dominant mega-corporate political class narrative of issues and events, secondly, a reform narrative providing useful information.

While, the importance of a free press has always been understood for self-government, in the era of the networked micro-processor, another element has been added, that of editor of the oceans of information being created. There is a great advantage provided by size in such an environment. If you know what you're looking for, greater and greater amounts of specific valued information become useful. However, if you're an individual on the receiving end of greater and greater amounts of information, you're at a disadvantage for finding what is valuable, or increasingly at the mercy of mega-corporate editing. This is particularly true in what we define as traditional political news, which for example crosses our screens at the speed of light without our being able to truly discern, unless we have previous knowledge, the difference in its importance for our daily lives, say of the solvency of Greece or the latest sexual scandal of any public official.

A successful reform communications network is going to have to place grave importance on editing and providing context. This can be done through, call them participatory information associations, comprised of individuals and nodes across the network. In many ways, the centralized editorial control, say of Google, is a problem brought forward from two inherited forms. The first is the industrial corporation itself. The second is newer, but just as problematic, the bringing forward and continued dominance of the original "client/server" model of networked computing. Two decades ago, Mitch Kapor (founder of Lotus Development) correctly defined an essential political element of our developing networked-microprocessor world stating, "Architecture is politics." Peer to peer technology and peer to peer editing, is the architecture of a democratic reform politics.

4. DEFLATION

In the modern industrial era, there have been three great deflationary periods. The late 19th century American Populist era, the Great Depression era, and Japan of the past two decades. Deflation remains not very well understood. Each era has some similarities but also great differences. Money definitely plays a role, but how much as cause, opposed to effect, is very much open to debate. At this point, money as prime cause dominates established economic thinking. However, massive societal and/or global deflations have represented much greater problems than just questions on the quantity of money. They represent fundamental imbalances and changes in an economy, driven in large part by technology. Just as the deflationary eras of the past, our present challenges will not be met without addressing these greater issues of political economy.

The greatest barrier to a more encompassing and valuable understanding of deflation is the almost complete dominance of monetary thinking in all things economic. There hasn't been a great episode of deflation in the United States since the Depression. In the 1970s, much accepted thinking on money was supplanted, when it proved ineffectual in meeting the challenges of America's greatest inflationary era. Into the breach stepped monetarism, and for the past 30 years monetary thinking has been not simply dominant, but dictatorial in its rule. How this came about is both important and easier to understand in a political sense than a pseudo-scientific economic sense. At the center of the story stands one of American history's greatest and most destructive propagandists, Milton Friedman.

With a revisionist view of the causes of the Depression, Mr. Friedman rose to fame in the early 1960s. He laid all blame at the feet of the Fed, writing,

> "The Fed was largely responsible for converting what might have been a garden-variety recession, although perhaps a fairly severe one, into a major catastrophe. Instead of using its powers to offset the depression, it presided over a decline in the quantity of money by one-third from 1929 to 1933... Far from the depression being a failure of the free-enterprise system, it was a tragic failure of government."

Lucky for Milton, we had no deflation for the next 40 years to prove his theories wrong. However, it is necessary to understand Mr. Friedman's political objectives, which he states in the last sentence. They are key to understanding how an obscure academic from the University Chicago could become a major political figure riding a cockamamie revisionist theory of the Depression. Friedman's real objective was political, to loosen the power of Wall Street and the mega-corporations, which were briefly constrained by reforms of the New Deal. With financial backing from these entities, Mr. Friedman, his allies, and followers gained academic, media, and political power, fundamentally redefining and restructuring political economy in the United States over the last thirty years. Nonetheless, despite his overwhelming impact in all these areas, when it comes to deflation, Mr. Friedman's thinking still offers few solutions.

It's easy to see how one can honestly misconstrue money as the greatest factor in deflation, but this is both a historical misreading of events and just as importantly a graver barrier to necessary solutions. One thing the three great deflations have in common is that they were all preceded by great financial bubbles. However, these bubbles were much more than simple rises in the quantity of money, they represented great underlying distortions of the economy, both as attempts to keep a no longer sustainable status quo and heralding a rise of new economic structures driven by the adaption of new technology, thus requiring much bigger fixes than simple money manipulation.

This important dichotomy can best be represented by two men. First, Milton Friedman's greatest disciple, Alan Greenspan, who wrote in 1998,

"While asset price deflation can occur for a number of reasons, a persistent deflation in the prices of currently produced goods and services—just like a persistence a increase in these prices—necessarily is, at its root a monetary phenomenon."

As opposed to former Bank of Japan Governor Hayami, who in 2001, with ten years of deflationary experience wrote,

"At a time when prices decline on account of productivity gains based on rapid technological innovation, a forceful reduction in interest rates with a view to raising prices may amplify economic swings."

In these three deflationary eras, technological innovations have taken various forms and proved as important as money in defining the era. For example, in his seminal work on democracy in America, *The Populist Moment*, Lawrence Goodwyn writes,

> "In not the slightest way did silver address the accelerating movement toward industrial combination. As John D. Rockefeller has conclusively demonstrated in the course of creating the Standard Oil Trust, railroad networks were a central ingredient both in the combination movement itself and the political corruption that grew out of monopoly."

Money was an essential element to the Populist enterprise, but it was not alone, nor might it be argued, the greatest factor. The Populists were very much at war with the railroads, which in the 1870s and 1880s were completely destructing established American agrarian life. It is imperative to point out the Populists' concerns were not against rail technology, but against how it was controlled. In fact, in the Populists' famous 1892 Omaha Platform, the railroad plank is third, ahead of the finance plank,

> "Third.—We believe that the time has come when the railroad corporations will either own the people or the people must own the railroads, and should the government enter upon the work of owning and managing all railroads, we should favor an amendment to the Constitution by which all persons engaged in the government service shall be placed under a civil-service regulation of the most rigid character, so as to prevent the increase of the power of the national administration by the use of such additional government employees."

Note, importantly, how the Populists were very concerned with newly concentrated power in recommending turning control of the railroads over to the federal government. They insisted on a constitutional amendment to check and balance this new concentration of power. Unlike, many of their 21st century progeny, 19th century American citizens understood the democratic imperative of decentralized political power. Though advocating federal control as a solution to their railroad problem, they nonetheless remained greatly aware and disconcerted by the idea. The essential point is the Populists understood the importance of technology in creating their problems, thus included it in their solutions.

Fifty years later, technology played a tremendous role in the Depression's deflation. By the 1920s, the United States was rapidly changing with the implementation of mass electricity, broadcast media, and the automobile. The New Deal's political economy solutions, including establishment of unions, the great electrification projects, and the regulation, in retrospect, the very awful regulation of broadcast media by the federal government, all played as important roles as financial reform in getting the United States out of the Depression.

Today, we have new technologies, most importantly the networked microprocessor, fundamentally changing our political economy, particularly in helping foster the control necessary for corporate globalization. This process has greatly contributed to deflationary/stagnant economic environments in Japan, the US, and Europe. The role corporate globalization has played, especially in the development of China and other parts of East Asia, and the resulting impact on the Japanese export economy has not been given nearly enough attention as a cause of Japan's two-decades deflation problems.

In short, deflation is not simply a monetary problem, and thus will not simply be solved with monetary solutions. We need massive financial and monetary reform in this country and across the planet, but they alone will not be sufficient to meeting the challenges facing our greater political economy. We need to fundamentally restructure our entire political economy.

5. SYSTEMS THINKING

"In fact Anaximander had a geometric image of the universe. The elements, however they struggled and whatever forms they assumed, had to be in some kind of equilibrium, an "equality of power." All of them derived ultimately from the infinite indeterminate substance which he called *apeiron*, a neutral material from which binary oppositions emerged: dark and light, hot and cold, dry and wet, thick and thin, as well as Water, Vapor, and Fire. These elements in turn combined to give rise to living creatures, plants, animals, humans, according to a natural order whereby not one element dominated the others in form of *dunasteia* or *monarchia*. A doctor and Pythagorean philosopher, Alcmeon, repeated in the early 5th century the image which by then had become commonplace that "health was a balance of powers, *insonomia ton dunameon*, while sickness resulted on the contrary from the domination of one element over the others.""

"In short, this was a view of the cosmos without hierarchy, where no one element fully obeyed another, a world in which conflicts balanced, reminding us irresistibly of the social and political structure of the *polis*. Government was no longer in the hands of gods or kings but in the hands of men who had equal rights. Anaximander's universe reflected the idealized equilibrium of the city-state. The world view changed because the world had changed and it became possible to project the everyday world on to the cosmos. J.-P. Vernant sums it up as follows: "When Aristotle defines man as political animal, he is pointing to something that differentiates Reason in the Greek sense from that of our time. If in his eyes *Homo sapiens* was *Homo politicus*, that was because Reason was itself political in essence." —Fernand Braudel, *Memory and the Mediterranean*

"Systems thinking" is a school of thought developed in the 20th century. Its influence has not been great, mostly impacting thinking on the environment, biology, some physics, and in some information/communications thought. Yet in politics, the area it could prove of the most immediate and beneficial value, systems thinking has little influence whatsoever. Adopting systems thinking would provide a framework to help us begin the necessary reform of our political economy.

Despite seeming quite obvious, systems thinking is in many ways a radical addition to what has become the adopted and accepted methods of scientific reason. The two main components of reasoning in the great scientific revolution of the past five-centuries are reductionism and determinism. Reductionism simply defined as dividing a system into its basic elements. Determinism defined as once you establish these elements and their interactions, certain outcomes can be concluded.

Simplistically, systems thinking can be defined with the old expression, the whole is greater than the sum of the parts. Systems thinking asks how components interact as a whole, with the understanding by looking at the whole, we gain additional insights and values. In fact, the system as a whole can determine certain actions of the parts, helping define the parts themselves.

In human society, politics and government must provide a systems view. Historically in the United States, we can look back to the unanimous view of the founders that government, "a more perfect union" was established for the "common defense" and the "general welfare." However, simultaneous with the founding of the American republic, the industrial era birthed, based on technology developed by the scientific revolution's reason, and it dominated the shaping of society to a far greater degree than the new experiment in self-government.

This process of shaping is best described by Adam Smith in *The Wealth of Nations*, particularly the description of the "division of labor." Smith documented the division of labor in the burgeoning manufacturing sectors—the physically applied scientific methods of reductionism and determinism.

What Smith failed to realize was the division of labor, over time, would also become the division of learning and intellect. With industrialization, an increasingly technologically complex society became pervasive. The systems values of production/consumption supplanted and dominated all others. Industrial thinking and technique shaped every aspect of society, including education, politics, and government. However, in *The Wealth of Nations*, Smith himself recognizes the importance of systems thinking writing,

"All the improvements in machinery, however, have by no means been the inventions of those who had occasion to use the machines. Many improvements have been made by the ingenuity of the makers of the machines, when to make them became the business of a peculiar trade; and some by that of those who are called philosophers or men of speculation, whose trade it is not to do any thing, but to observe everything, and who, upon that account, are often capable of combining together the powers of the most distant and dissimilar objects. In the progress of society, philosophy, or speculation becomes, like every other employment, the principal or the sole trade and occupation of a particular class of citizens. Like every other employment too, it is subdivided into a great number of different branches, each of which affords occupation to a particular tribe or call of philosophers; and this subdivision at employment in philosophy, as well as in every other business, improves dexterity and saves time. Each individual becomes more expert in his own peculiar branch, more work is done upon the whole, and quantity of science is considerably increased by it."

Yet, Smith segregates systems thinking into just another reductionist component of the industrial system. Industrial society continued this dividing and reducing over the next two centuries. Today, any sort of systems view, for example, gained from a liberal arts education, or from politics and government, is devalued to the point of meaninglessness. In education, this has meant the devaluing of a liberal arts or catholic education, replaced with the totality of specialization. While in politics and government, it has meant the division and specialization of elected officials, staff, bureaucracy, and of course the fantastic growth in specialized lobbying.

In order to revive and reform our politics and government, we need to begin including other systems views, thus undertaking a revaluing. Looking at society with additional systems perspectives will enable us to reevaluate, revalue, and redesign the components of our political economy. In establishing a reform politics using systems thinking, several strongly present themselves as imperative for humanity's near and long term future; geography/environment/planet, energy, information/communications, and decision making/power.

" In the folk image of space and time, man is at the center of a very cozy little universe which surrounds him. In the scientific image, man is an occupant of a minute planet revolving around a minor sun in an insignificant and remote arm of a commonplace galaxy in a billion-galaxied universe. This change may be deeply disturbing to man's self-respect unless it goes along with a certain shift in his values toward a deeper humility than he has usually achieved." —Kenneth Boulding, *The Meaning of the 20th Century*

Geography/environment/planet is a systems view that is ancient, but has been redefined and transcended by the scientific and industrial revolutions. For the vast majority of human history, geography heterogeneously defined much of human culture, including everything from the food system, buildings, and religion. Too little appreciated by contemporary understanding is the phenomena of the industrial era transcending geographic constraints, eliminating diversity, and homogenizing human life around various technologies. As industrialization spread across the globe, a planetary political system evolved, seen in its most developed and nefarious form with the rise of corporate globalization.

With this technological transcending of geography came a growing planetary awareness, most sublimely, in the last half-century for the first time in human history, the majority of earth's inhabitants awareness that we inhabit a relatively small planet orbiting an unexceptional star. Where this awareness will eventually lead is little understood, but it allows and imperatively necessitates one of the most important new systems view in human history, the planet.

The final systems thinking in this troika is the environment, for most of human history defined largely by a culture's specific geographic location. However, in the last century, local environments were reshaped and even destroyed by technology. Paradoxically, an awareness is growing that environmental systems are very much defined by the planetary system itself. For the last half-century, systems thinking about the environment has offered the greatest challenge to our dominant production/consumption value system, though with extremely limited impact.

Thinking and technology created using reductionism and determinism allows a systems view of the planet, creating the need for new systems thinking. We can start with the understanding technologies create environments of their own, and instead of trying to transcend and exploit systems, which evolved the species homo sapiens, we need to develop technologies that compliment them. Instead of trying to supplant heterogeneous local geographies and environments, we can learn to evolve technologies aligned with the specific advantages of locality.

> "An anti-entropic technology is on the way—that is one which will concentrate diffused material rather than diffusing the concentrated." —Kenneth Boulding

The harnessing of fossil fuels, coal first, then oil, and now increasingly natural gas, beyond any other industrial development defines the modern age. In recent decades from a planetary systems view, it has become clear due to environmental impact, constraints in supply, and ever expanding population growth, we will soon meet the limits of the fossil fuel age. Arguably, there is no greater present systems challenge than restructuring our fossil fuel energy system and the physical infrastructure it created. In fact, it can be argued this infrastructure, once considered the pinnacle of development, increasingly will be a burden, so much so, it may be said those who have a limited fossil fuel based infrastructure may well have certain advantages toward the future.

The present energy system is so integral and deeply ingrained in every aspect of modern society it is mind-numbing to begin addressing, though looking from a systems level provides a catalyzing perspective. The values of the production/consumption system have been foremost in building and running our fossil fuel energy system. The values of cheap price, unlimited supply, and unlimited growth were the wrong values for something with such fundamental importance. We need to raise the price of fossil fuels to begin creating a new energy infrastructure based not on unlimited amounts, but enough. The foremost systemic change will be moving from extracting mass amounts of energy from the concentrated energy sources of fossil fuels to gathering specific amounts of energy from dispersed sources such as solar, wind, and the tides.

"By this conversion of political privilege into a provision for the poor, a principle remarkable in a moral as well as in a historical point of view came for the first time into living operation. Civil society but slowly and gradually works its way to a perception of the interdependence of interests; in earlier antiquity the state doubtless protected its members from the public enemy and the murderer, but it was not bound to protect the totally helpless fellow-citizen from the worse enemy, want, by affording the needful means of subsistence." —Theodor Mommsen, *History of Rome*

The final two systems views, information/communications and decision making/power are inseparable. The foundation of the past five-centuries scientific revolution is the creation of information and its dissemination through communication. Over much of this time, the information medium was predominantly paper, specifically the book, while its transference speed was limited to a horse's gallop. In the 19th century, with the invention of the telegraph, information began its transformation into electric media, communicated at the speed of light.

Today, the networked microprocessor allows the creation and communication of information in literally astronomical amounts, initiating changes to society as radical as those of the industrial era. Already, this transformation begins to reform the production/consumption paradigm with, amongst other things, the automation of labor. More important and less understood, what was always the physical impossibility of unlimited growth in industrial doctrine, becomes an actuality regarding information and communication. However, though the creation of information and its communication may very well be infinite, for it to be useful, it must be edited.

Presently, we are attempting to graft production/consumption values, processes, and institutions onto new information/communications systems. A century ago, industry and its processes displaced millenia old agrarian values and institutions. Today, information/communication systems begin to define 21st century political economy. Just as the corporation, labor, commodities and energy defined industrial system values, developing information/communications values: creation, editing, communication, control, associations, and finally decision making, will define this era.

Just as our energy system must use more anti-entropic technologies, so too our political economy must embrace anti-entropic politics, that is democracy. The real value in the system of information and its communication is going to be in allowing every individual to participate in all its aspects—*e pluribus unum*. For the fact is, the most anti-entropic force in the universe is life, in all its forms and brevity. Democracy is the politics of life.

And while the structure, the architecture of these systems, defines power, the essential political element—decision making—will be key to understanding how we reform. At present, decision making in the industrial era corporation is autocratic, while our government decision making is hierarchical, with a few representative and democratic inputs—all are increasingly dysfunctional. Asking how our political economy, with sophisticated information/communications systems, fosters democratic decision making will help guide the design of the system as a whole.

"A genuine revolution of values means in the final analysis that our loyalties must become ecumenical rather than sectional. Every nation must now develop an overriding loyalty to mankind as a whole in order to preserve the best in their individual societies. This call for a worldwide fellowship that lifts neighborly concern beyond one's tribe, race, class, and nation is in reality a call for an all-embracing, unconditional love for all men." —Martin Luther King, Jr.

Including systems thinking in our politics allows us to gain perspective for the necessary reforming, reshaping, and evolution of our political economy. In the end, we are not so far from the Ancient Greeks. We know much more science, allowing us to create an ever more complex technological society, which would no doubt astound the ancients. However, we have lost a certain wisdom the Greeks possessed, in the design and conduct of human affairs, in all its aspects, reason itself is political.

VI. REFORMING POLITICAL ECONOMY

1. AN ECONOMIC REFORMATION

Karl Polanyi's, The Great Transformation is a truly original and important work published in 1944. Polanyi doesn't fit well in our standard left/right economic dichotomy and for the refined economic tastes of the past several decades, he includes far too much history and politics. Most contemporary economists would no doubt shake their heads and say, "How can a book about economics be taken seriously, when it doesn't have one equation?" That would be a great mistake. Mr. Polanyi's insights deserve great attention.

Polanyi wrote The Great Transformation during World War II. With depression and war, the previous two decades had been a cataclysmic time for the planet. His central thesis was, "The origins of the cataclysm lay in the utopian endeavor of economic liberalism to set up a self-regulating market system." The book decisively pooh-poohs many of the myths of our ruling economic doctrine.

Most importantly, he eviscerates the idea of laissez-faire and uniquely documents Europe's century and half revolution to a market society. Time after time, Polanyi shows the very visible hand of the government interfering in all aspects of society in order to insure market dominance.

Now this point is especially relevant to us today. For the last several decades, we have witnessed a resurgence of economic liberalism—neo-liberalism. We were told once again that markets could self-regulate, and once again it has come crashing down. Most importantly, over the last several years, we've watched government step in to save some of our largest market institutions, including the locus of laissez-faire, Wall Street itself.

Polanyi is not anti-market. He believes they are indeed beneficial, but they are not self-regulating, and more importantly the ethos of the market should not be the ruling or even dominant ethic of society. The idea of self-regulating markets is utopian, and like all utopias extremely brutal if tried to be realized.

It would take a long piece to give Mr. Polanyi an overview his thinking deserves. However, there are a few points in Mr. Polanyi's book that I'd like to emphasize because of their relevance for today's financial crisis. First, regarding the financial collapse of the late 1920s and early 1930s, Polanyi writes:

"In the 1920s, the gold standard was still regarded as *the* precondition of a return to stability and prosperity, and consequently no demand raised by its professional guardians, the bankers, was deemed too burdensome, if only it promised to secure stable exchange rates; when, after 1929, this proved impossible, the imperative need was for a stable internal currency and nobody was as little qualified to provide it as the banker."

This is terribly important today. If you simply replace the gold standard with our "financial innovations" of the last few decades, we have a very similar situation. In the last year and half, every action taken by the Federal Reserve and Treasury has been an attempt to return to the "stability" of the last decades' casino banking of derivatives and securitization. This isn't going to work. Just like then, the bankers who provided us with securitization and derivatives are the least qualified to bring about the changes we are in such desperate need.

Secondly, Polanyi astutely points out the necessity of locality. This insight deserves a great deal of thought. It is an important component of our current banking problems. It provides an important principle for the necessary political reform that must accompany any real reform of our banking sector. Polanyi writes,

> "In contrast to the nomadic peoples, the cultivator commits himself to improvements fixed in a particular place. Without such improvements human life must remain elementary, and little removed from that of animals. And how large a role have these fixtures played in human history! It is they, the cleared and cultivated lands, the other buildings, the means of communication, the multifarious plant necessary for production, including industry and mining, all permanent and immovable improvements that tie a human community to the locality where it is. They cannot be improvised, but must be built up gradually by generations of patient effort, and the community cannot afford to sacrifice them and start afresh elsewhere. Hence that territorial character of sovereignty, which permeates our political conceptions—for a century these obvious truths were ridiculed."

Once again, over the last several decades, these obvious truths were ridiculed. In short, power must in some ways remain tied to locality. It cannot all be centralized and globalized. Centralization is both the enemy of locality and of democracy. Yet, over the last several decades, the centralizing of the American economy under a utopian free-market fundamentalism has been staggering. The *Fi-*

nancial Times writes, "The four biggest US commercial banks—JP-Morgan Chase, Citigroup, Bank of America and Wells Fargo—possess 64 per cent of the assets of US commercial banks."

When power becomes so concentrated it devolves certain traits. One of the most important of these traits in recent years has been the growing use of mathematical models, no more so rampant than in the banking sector. Yves Smith has touched on the issue as it relates to the mortgage fiasco stating quite accurately,

> "The problem is that there isn't a good substitute for knowledge of the borrower and his community. Does he understand what he is getting into? How stable is his employer? What are the prospects for the local economy? Those are important considerations, and they require judgment. That may still in the end be used as an input to a more structured decision process but overly automating borrower assessment has resulted in information loss. It's hardly a surprise that the quality of decisions deteriorated."

Of course, modeling is not exclusive to the banking sectors. It has become essential in many of our large corporations and just as important in our centralized government bureaucracies. We need to step back from this headlong rush, this modern Pythagorean movement of enshrining mathematics. We must rethink our institutions of political economy away from centralization and the seductive but wrong-headed notion of ever more efficient control from the top. Both practices are antithetical to democracy.

Instead, we need to reform our institutions of political economy, not based on mathematical models, don't misunderstand, they still can be useful tools, but instead founded on the principles that people with all their human complexities and the localities in which they live and work must always be preeminent. We must understand that in order to create truly adaptive systems of political economy, which grow ever more necessary with the evolution of technology, we must allow our political economy to evolve and adapt. Centralization is not only the least conducive and the least democratic to these means, it eventually becomes truly reactionary.

In 1944, Polanyi had lived through the great cataclysms brought about by self-regulating market utopia. With the rise of the New Deal and the defeat of fascism, Polanyi thought he was witnessing, "a development which the economic system ceases to lay down the law to society and primacy of society over that system is secured." Yet four decades later, the myth of the market once again rules and has led once again led to crisis.

We need to learn from this. Over the longer term the New Deal failed to keep markets restrained. While providing short-term relief, over time, the centralization of political power in DC proved as problematic as centralization of economic power in our megacorporations. The corporations were easily able to take over the government. Those today who wish to once again confront the myths of self-regulating markets also need to confront the challenge of reforming our politics and government. Mr. Polanyi offers some valuable thinking.

* * *

"Nowadays people know the price of everything and the value of nothing." —Oscar Wilde, *The Picture of Dorian Gray*

The Value of Nothing is a good critique of our present political economy and gives an incisive look of how it came to be, where we are now, and begins an essential look at some ideas and practices on how we begin to evolve a more sustainable and satisfying political economy.

We are in need not of revolution, but of reformation. When a ruling doctrine becomes ubiquitous across a society, it is difficult for members of the society to imagine any alternative. The doctrine comes to define all aspects of life, and facts are interpreted not for what they say, but for how they support the ruling doctrine, even if they don't. Raj Patel's *The Value of Nothing* offers an excellent historical look at how "free-market" doctrine and institutions came to dominate our lives. From Adam Smith to Karl Polanyi, Patel shows how free market philosophy redefined human culture, while the doctrine of laissez faire relied totally on government to be instituted.

The pinnacle of free market thought was reached in the last several decades with efficient market theory, which led to the retreat of even minimal government oversight in the affairs of mega-corporations. This, as Patel points out, led to the recent financial disaster, which in the halls of power and the vestibules of our free market temples, has yet to lead to any serious rethinking. An interesting point Patel brings up is how the top of the system, Wall Street, is now inundated with data in the belief this gives them knowledge. He writes, "Data pelting down monitors is what the masters of the universe on the global financial exchanges stare at, their eyes darting from screen to screen, trying to see through the world and profit from it."

This made me think how our present circumstances are much different from the 1930s. In Keynes' *A Treatise on Money*, he constantly laments the lack of data available, it being a hindrance for making any definitive judgment on his equations or theories. (As an aside, this should give rise to great skepticism on what people today say they learned from the data poor 1930s.) What *The Value of Nothing* reveals is it isn't the data that is the problem today, but the categories, equations, and theories we are plugging the data into.

Over several centuries, markets and market theory have run ramshackle over every other social institution. We no longer have the ability to value anything outside market terms, because the institutions and social constructs to do so, have all been eliminated or subverted. We are Patel states simply "homo economicus," look-ing and acting from only one perspective. In doing so, we are not simply mis-pricing but devaluing some of the most basic necessi-ties of homo sapiens, most importantly food and the environment. It is not us or flawed markets that are the determinant of these val-ues, but mega-corporations who hold the most influence, and cor-porate power is not a factor in our ruling economic theory.

How do we become more full human beings is the essential and necessary question of *The Value of Nothing*. And at a time where the most fundamental tenet of industrial capitalism, unlimited growth, is meeting its limits and causing havoc with the practice of unbridled consumption, Patel offers food for thought: "The oppo-site of consumption isn't thrift—it's generosity."

The Value of Nothing provides examples in the developing world, which are in the midst of overturning their old institutions and thus their values, replacing them with the institutions and the values of markets. It gives examples of how people are stand-ing-up. Will the global south be where we evolve new institutions and thought to cope with the realities of the 21st century? *The Value of Nothing* shows we must reform and evolve our institu-tions. Our democratic infrastructure, be it government, political, or social institutions have been quashed or are in disrepair. The solu-tion to our economic problems is not better economic theory, but a democratic revival, a revaluation of value.

* * *

"Each new fact in his private experience flashes a light on what great bodies of men have done, and the crises of his life refer to national crises. Every revolution was first a thought in one man's mind, and when the same thought occurs to another man, it is the key to that era. Every reform was once a private opin-ion, and when it shall be a private opinion again, it will solve the problem of the age." —Ralph Waldo Emerson, *History*

Chapters of history are in part composed of tales concerning the rise and fall of nations. All contain verses of the times nations reached great heights and then faced serious challenges. Aspects of the culture, politics and economy, which brought the nation to its heights, are no longer sufficient to sustain the position reached. Principles and practices once used for achieving success are abandoned or corrupted, while new circumstances require genuinely new actions, ideas, and methods. In short, the nation faces an era of reform. A peoples' ability to meet this challenge defines their future, a future of either continued possibilities or decline.

Each nation's story, like every individual person's life, is different. However, all have similarities, some quite striking, offering us lessons from the past for the present. Such is the case with 17th century Spain for 21st century America. By the early 1600s, Spain faced an essential need for fundamental reform of their political economy, similar to what we face today. J.H. Elliott's, *The Count-Duke of Olivares: The Statesman in an Age of Decline* is an excellent history of the era, offering invaluable lessons on reform from a people who failed to meet the challenges set before them.

Spain's history is long and fascinating. One of the Roman Republic's first conquests outside of Italy, Spain fell under Rome's control in 200 BC, with the defeat of Carthage under their sublime general Hannibal. In the 8th century, Spain was conquered in the initial great wave of Muslim ascendancy, and in various ways remained under Muslim rule and influence for the next 700 years. In the mid-15th century, the uniting of the Christian kingdoms of Castile and Aragon launched Spain into a high period of cultural, economic and political power lasting roughly a century and half.

In this period, Spain would discover the New World and conquer the great civilizations of the Aztecs in Mexico and the Inca in Peru, keeping the Spanish treasury flush with gold and silver. The Spanish monarchy's matrimonial alliance with the Holy Roman Empire's Austrian Hapsburgs would give Spain control of parts of

Europe, including the Netherlands and Belgium. The 16th century Spanish empire was one of Europe's and the world's greatest powers.

Nonetheless, by the beginning of the 17th century, many of the things that had previously made Spain great began to cause them problems. The empire drained wealth instead of increasing it. The Netherlands was in open revolt, and maybe most importantly the easy money from America, that had drastically changed the Spanish economy, began drying up. Elliott describes these economic changes in a way that would be familiar to any contemporary American,

> "Seventeenth-century Castile was a rentier society, with people at many social levels drawing a substantial portion of their annual income from *rentas*, in the form of annuities on state bonds (*juros*) and individual or corporate bonds (*censos*). Rates of return varied. ...But the underlying problems remained. The crown had a staggering burden of indebtedness; and in the opinion of the Council of Finance, one of the major reasons for the decline of industry and agriculture in Castile was the availability of *juros* and *censos* "at such advantageous rates that their yield is considered to be higher than the profits to be made in trade, agriculture, and stockraising." The result was that people tried to live on annuities, instead of using their capital for more forms of investment."

The great wealth produced by an extensive global network, and the easy money policies provided by the massive influx of New World gold and silver, produced both the hollowing and the financialization of the Spanish economy. Over time, real wealth was no longer created in Spain, just debt, which for a short time can be confused with wealth, until the debt comes due.

With such a change in political economy comes a necessary change in the power structure. Elliott describes,

"The late sixteenth century therefore saw the acceleration of a process that was to cast a long shadow over the future history of Castile—the consolidation of a rentier oligarchy of *pederosos* (powerful ones), who took advantage of the needs of the crown and distress of the peasantry to concentrate land, jurisdiction and revenues overwhelming into their own hands. The oligarchy was drawn from the ranks of the nobility and the urban patriciates, of the upper echelons of the bureaucracy, and of the wealthy peasant proprietors who knew how to play the market."

If you replace *pederosos* with Wall Street and mega-corporations, the oligarchy with our political class, and the peasantry with working America, you get a pretty good description of power in our own political economy.

In 1621, the sixteen-year old Philip IV would ascend to the monarchy and appoint the Count-Duke of Olivares to be his chief minister, a position Olivares would hold for the next two decades. Olivares was part of the Spanish nobility who understood that far from the great and enduring power Spain seemed to be at the time, they had reached a necessary point of reform.

Olivares understood the tremendous challenges Spain faced, both systemic and a problem of personnel. In regards to the latter, one of the previous king's ministers, Santamaria describes the situation best,

"The corruption from which the monarchy was at present suffering was a result of the wickedness and inadequacy of the men who governed it... Philip must act at once to 'clean out the entire fishpond'. He must get rid of the men who had deceived his father and had packed the palace with their creatures and confidants—all of them men who were 'unworthy and ridiculous, in Spain and outside of it.'"

Olivares boiled the problem down to this simple understanding and solution,

"Reformation meant a vigorous drive against every kind of fraud; it meant educating the new generation to place the public interest ahead of its own."

In Olivares' twenty-year rule, he would struggle continuously and ineffectively with this problem. While he somewhat successfully carried out a swapping-out of personnel, the greater problems were systemic. The Spanish monarchy was still a conglomeration of semi-independent sovereigns with centuries old powers, traditions, and methods. Olivares attempted to reform government power, usually trying to end-run established ways. For example, with his creation of a *Junta De Reformacion*, Olivares sought to maneuver around the entrenched power of the royal court. At other times, he created new power for local authorities, such as new banks, in order to get around a corrupted and effete nobility. Yet, these reforms turned out to be halfhearted and insufficient to meet the structural challenges facing the political economy.

By the beginning of the 17th century, the empire was massively draining wealth. Increasingly, the crown could not meet its bills. The hollowing of the domestic economy limited tax revenues and increased reliance on imports. The cheap money provided by the supplies of New World gold and silver, to which the economy was ever more dependent due to increased financialization, shrank in abundance each year. There's an amusing story of how in 1631 a great financial crisis was instigated by the Dutch seizing the annual gold and silver flotilla sailing from Mexico.

Spain's military entanglements, particularly the costs of trying to keep the Dutch subjugated, grew to be an ever greater burden on the royal treasury. These war burdens would vex Olivares his entire time in office. Tragically, he only added to the problem by getting into fights with the French, particularly an ill-advised campaign in Italy. More than any other single factor, these unsustainable military costs proved the greatest burden to accomplishing any true reform.

The decline of the economy coupled with growing military expenditures created an increasingly heavy tax burden, falling most heavily on the lowest rungs of the economic ladder. Unable to enact real reforms fast or sufficient enough, Olivares turned to manipulating the money supply, unaware or ignoring the fact that money's deterioration was a direct result of the problems in the real physical economy.

The Spanish money supply was divided into two currencies, silver and copper. Silver was held mostly by the aristocracy and used for trade and funding the military. While in the form of the *vellon* coin, copper was the main currency of the domestic economy. Overnight in 1628, Olivares reduced the value of the *vellon* by half, creating a little short-term relief, followed in the future by further ineffective money manipulations. Eight years later, Elliott writes of another change in monetary policy,

> "Accompanied as it were by harvest failure, the monetary confusion of 1636 had a drastic impact on the wage-earners, and the next two or three years wiped out half the gain in real wages that they had made in the preceding seven. But, as the war made the poor poorer, so it created spectacular opportunities for others to grow rich. The crown's bankers, the military entrepreneurs, strategically placed ministers and royal officials, tax-collectors, the administrators of royal rents and the poderosos of the towns and villages—all saw an opportunity in the crown's embarrassments to feather already well-feathered nests."

And thus, the Spanish economy remained firmly in the claws of the financial and political classes. In an attempt to loose the wealth of the nobility for the good of the greater economy, Olivares would unsuccessfully initiate various banking reforms, even to almost universal domestic consternation, bringing in the hated international financiers, the Genoese. Nothing proved successful. The financial class and political classes pushed ever greater burdens on those below, leading in the 1830s to revolts around Spain. Elliott, writing of one such revolt in the Basque region, concludes,

> "The Bilbao riots can be seen at one level as an uprising in defence of traditional Basque liberties. But at another they constituted a movement of popular protest against the domination of the region's life by an entrenched oligarchy—by town councilors, and rich merchants and the local nobility, who formed and intricate network of power and patronage."

In the early 1640s with Spain now at war with France, and the crown facing ever greater economic uncertainty, Olivares was run from office. His reforms had failed, and though many things he attempted were tried again in the coming decades, the Spanish Empire was set on the road to a long slow decline. Elliott concludes,

> "To reverse the trajectory of a nation through revolution from above demands a high degree of discontinuity, with all the consequent strains on the fabric of society. In the circumstances of the seventeenth century the kind of social engineering required to produce such discontinuity was neither intellectually conceivable nor within the realms of administrative possibility. The ordering of society was God-given and its vision of the future was bounded by the veneration of the past. At best, the would-be reformer could do little more than seek to purge excesses, remove abuses, and introduce more or less piecemeal certain administrative, economic and institutional changes which might with the passage of time to help to modify or alter the attitudes of the society at large."

Clearly 17th century Spain faced many similar challenges the United States faces at the beginning of the 21st. We have an economy that has become increasingly financialized and centralized, unsustainable military burdens, and a dysfunctional and corrupt political system. We can learn from the failures of Olivares, most importantly that all movements for reform must be both resolute and significant. Other lessons we can take from Olivares' experiences include "When there are systemic political economy problems, simply swapping-out personnel is insufficient."

Power is zero-sum. You have to fight and take from established power in order to implement reform. You cannot make them happy, they will be angry. In another era of reform, Franklin Roosevelt replied to the wails of entrenched power, "I welcome their hatred."

When you have problems with the physical economy, no amount of manipulation of the monetary system is going to change things, unless you simultaneously fix the problems of the physical economy. If a system is centralized, dysfunctional, and corrupt, the essential and primary action of reform is to break-up and distribute power.

This last point, optimistically separates us from 17th century Spain. Combining this point with Elliott's insight of Spanish reform being hampered by veneration of the past, an inability to imagine distributing power from established hierarchy, we fully see our advantage. Our republic was born in rebellion against entrenched hierarchy. Whether it is too much corrupt and dysfunctional power in DC, on Wall Street, or in our mega-corporations, the most essential element of reform, breaking up and distributing power is part of the blood coursing the veins of this republic's body politic. It flows in each of us.

2. PLANET ECONOMICS

It's sometimes seductive to think of the African wild as the last frontier, but that would be wrong. Across the entire continent, the wild areas of Africa are under severe pressure. The human population of sub-Saharan Africa is quickly nearing one billion people. American, European, and now Chinese interests exploit Africa's natural resources.

This doesn't leave much room for error in human affairs or change in environmental conditions to initiate decimation for much of the remaining animal populations. For example, lion populations across Africa have crashed in the last two decades from 200,000 to less than 20,000, over 90% decline in 20 years.

We will not preserve what's left of the African wild without helping the people of Africa. Unfortunately, for those concerned in the United States, and we all need to be, our experience in preserving wildlife isn't great. Despite the undeniable beauty of some of our national parks, outside of Alaska and we're still working on that, we didn't save enough space to keep the vast animal populations still seen in areas of Africa.

More importantly, our development model is largely irrelevant to Africa. We are five percent of the world and use 25% of the world's resources. Here are some numbers to understand exactly what that means. Kenya has 40 million people, roughly the population of California. The Kenyan economy is $30 billion a year, California's is $1.7 trillion. Kenyan GDP per capita is $1700 a year, while California's is $42,000. But the figure most telling in understanding today's global disparities is energy use, even more so in recent years as climate change has become the focus of northern environmentalists. Kenya's electricity use is 1.6% that of California's.

Kenya, sub-Saharan Africa, and the rest of the developing world are going to have to come up with different development models. There are simply not enough resources on a finite planet for 7 billion people to live an American consumer lifestyle. Indeed, there are not enough resources for 300 million Americans to live late 20th century consumer lifestyles. Luckily, alternatives are developing. A little solar energy would go a long way in providing an infrastructure for non-fossil fuel development and a sustainable future for the people and animals of Africa.

* * *

Twenty years ago, I had the great privilege of spending some time in Gunung Leuser, the last of Sumatra's once great wild. The final leg of the trip was on a bus, the drive-shaft dropped half-way. It wasn't the first or last time I was on a bus that dropped its drive shaft onto the road. I stayed with Mr. Jolli in his tobacco hut on the northern border, which is just as it sounds, one room, thatched roof, perched above the wet ground on six-foot stilts, just at the farmed edge of the forest. I went there to see one thing, the "man of the forest," and after numerous treks through sublime old forest, I saw an orangutan. I smelled her first actually, which is many times the case with large beasties. She was beautiful, lounging 30 feet in the tops of the tree, coming down to about six feet, to investigate the yapping of a little mongrel dog, who had uninvited, joined us on one of our treks.

So, it's sad, but completely understandable to read in The Independent, that one of the last refuges of the orangutan is being destroyed for palm oil. Indonesia is the greatest producer of palm oil, mostly for foodstuffs, but increasingly promoted by many softheads for "bio-diesel," a sin we know well.

As an American, it is difficult to point an accusatory finger at conservation issues anywhere else in the world. In 200 years, we've not done much, particularly when it comes to keeping space for large non-human mammals.

More important are the numbers, though I'm not sure how useful numbers are with innumerate America, especially amongst bankers and economists, certainly accounting has no value. Nonetheless, let us push forward remembering, Sisyphus was always smiling. Indonesia has 250 million people. It's per capita GDP is $4,200, compared to the United States' $47,000, almost 12 times as great. If Indonesia, less than five percent of the world was to have an equivalent GDP as the US, it would require an increase in total global resources of over 20%! This of course has been the fundamental lie of corporate globalization—that the world could live like hyper-consumptive Americans. And don't believe Al Gore that global warming is the greatest environmental problem, there are others, plenty, as they like to say in East Africa. Make no mistake America, on a global resource level, we're all the 1%.

3. THE INFORMATION ECONOMY AND THE END OF LABOR

"In the last twenty years an increasing percentage of our people have come to depend on industry for their livelihood, so that to-day the wage-workers in industry rank in importance side by side with the tillers of the soil. As a people we cannot afford to let any group of citizens or any individual citizen live or labor under conditions which are injurious to the common welfare... We must protect the crushable elements at the base of our present industrial structure."

"We stand for a living wage. Wages are subnormal if they fail to provide a living for those who devote their time and energy to industrial occupations. The monetary equivalent of a living wage varies according to local conditions, but must include enough to secure the elements of a normal standard of living—a standard high enough to make morality possible, to provide for education and recreation, to care for immature members of the family, to maintain the family during periods of sickness, and to permit a reasonable saving for old age.

"Hours are excessive if they fail to afford the worker sufficient time to recuperate and return to his work thoroughly refreshed. We hold that the night labor of women and children is abnormal and should be prohibited; we hold that the employment of women over forty-eight hours per week is abnormal and should be prohibited. We hold that the seven-day working week is abnormal, and we hold that one day of rest in seven should be provided by law. We hold that the continuous industries, operating twenty-four hours out of twenty-four, are abnormal, and where, because of public necessity or for technical reasons (such as molten metal), the twenty-four hours must be divided into two shifts of twelve hours or three shifts of eight, they should by law be divided into three of eight." —Theodore Roosevelt, 1912

Several decades ago, when I first went into electoral politics, I learned a lot from an old Democratic organizer. He used to say, "There's three planks to any Democratic campaign platform: Jobs, Jobs, and Jobs." That Democratic Party is a long time gone, replaced first by a massive capitulation to Reaganomics and then under the "leadership" of Robert Rubin and Bill Clinton to a party completely captured by the interests of Wall Street.

The social construct that is the job is increasingly insufficient to meet the political economy challenges of the 21st century. The above thoughts from a Teddy Roosevelt campaign speech give a little historical perspective. Today's social economic norms like the 40 hour work week, the 8 hour day, living wages etc. were developed over decades. The industrialization of America created an entirely new political economy vastly different from the agrarian/merchant political economy that dominated the republic's first hundred years. In fact, the job itself is an industrial era construct.

We are at the birth of a new era. We are discovering this transformation is as wrenching as the move from agrarian society to in-

dustrial society was a century ago. Presently, we remain firmly entrenched in the thinking of the industrial political economy. For
example, in the last four decades as Wall Street and our mega-corporations chased cheaper wages, closing and then shipping American industrial jobs across the globe, we commoditized other
segments of society to create replacement jobs. For example, we
created a massive "service" sector. Today, we don't need to create
more service sector jobs, in fact, we should get rid of many we
have, starting in the financial sector.

We need a new political economy, one based on the realities of
the 21st century. One that understands the evolution of technology, for example automating industry makes the number of new
jobs in even repatriated industries limited. Global resource constraints make it impossible for the other 95% of humanity to lead
the over-consumptive lives of contemporary Americans. All sorts
of environmental problems caused by industrial economy's quest
for infinite growth are severely impacting basic life systems necessary not simply for industrial society, but civilization as we know
it.

We will not meet these challenges by clinging to the beliefs,
constructs, and power structures of industrial political economy.
We can start by reevaluating the job, and we can start there by cutting the work week.

* * *

The continuation of the complete and total dominance of established economic orthodoxy remains unfathomable. At times, one
can only find encouragement in our gods. We can remember one
of the Twelve Labors of Heracles was to clean the Augean stables.
For the moment however, let's turn to Hannah Arendt, one of the
great minds of the 20th century and one of the greatest small "d"

democratic thinkers in history. In her book, *The Human Condition* Arendt puts forth this nugget about the impact on society of automating industry,

> "It is a society of laborers which is about to be liberated from the fetters of labor, and this society does no longer know of those other higher and more meaningful activities for the sake of which this freedom would be deserved to be won. Within this society, which is egalitarian because this is labor's way of making men live together, there is no class left, no aristocracy of either a political or spiritual nature from which a restoration of the other capacities of man could start anew. Even presidents, kings, and prime ministers think of their offices in terms of a job necessary for the life of society, and among intellectuals, only solitary individuals are left who consider what they are doing in terms of work and not in terms of making a living. What we are confronted with is the prospect of a society of laborers without labor, that is without the only activity left to them. Surely, nothing could be worse."

She wrote this in 1958, at the height of American industrial economy, and indeed, the height of American labor. However, she missed the development of the service or more accurately the "servants economy," in which many aspects of society were unnecessarily commoditized, in part to create new jobs for a society that was beginning to automate its industrial labor jobs. Missing this process, also caused Arendt to miss the reintroduction of class into American society and the creation of a neo-aristocracy, no matter how low and born into decadence it might be.

As unemployment approaches double digits and growth stagnates, there's one thing our political class shouts with one voice, "We need more jobs and more growth." This is the grail of industrial economics, but it's not going to happen. The majority of new jobs to be created in America are not going to provide people with any dignity, call it labor dignity if you like. And increasing industrial growth cannot be handled from the planet's perspective, nor even needed in already industrialized nations.

Instead of trying to figure out how we're going to create more jobs and growth, we need to concern ourselves with fixing our politics, and how we all become citizens. We need to create a participatory political infrastructure, educate, and give people time and space to be citizens. Most importantly, we as a society need to not simply value labor, but also value citizenry. This would begin to help us out of our labor dilemma.

4. THE DESIGN ECONOMY

I.

In contemporary economic discussion, the idea of the Industrial Revolution is frequently presented as something bland, neutral, and inevitable. Instead of conveying a sense of historical turmoil, disruption, and the overthrowing of established cultural, political, and economic institutions dating back millenia, we simply throw-off the term, "Industrial Revolution" with little regard that it represented a fundamental re-ordering of human life. In many ways this is understandable, as the Industrial Revolution triumphed, becoming industrial rule, industrial economy, industrial bureaucracy, and industrial life—the industrial status quo. In large swathes of the world, industrial economy is so dominant, it leaves the sense the world has always been that way and only a fool could imagine it being any different. Most amazingly, this has all been accomplished in less than two-centuries—an historical blink of the eye.

Today, we confront an era of equal historical change. Further understandings of the natural world and resulting new technologies are beginning to impact industrial society to a degree as fantastic as industrial knowledge and technology transformed agrarian society. While, agrarian civilization lasted over ten-thousand years, the reign of industrial society has been relatively brief, nonetheless, it is being usurped. This transformation is rapidly intruding on our lives, yet still not quite recognized beyond a general trepidation that things don't quite seem to work like they did before. The great collective social anxiety of the Industrial era, never satiated, now confronts a new transition for which the tools, skills, thinking and institutions are little developed, if they exist at all.

Maybe the most essential understanding we can have in such a time is the simple recognition of change. The Industrial era, for many reasons, is transitory. It is inherently unstable, and incapable of truly meeting the challenges and problems it created. For in the end, industrialism tries conforming or forcefully overwhelming life's great diversity into a few narrow homogeneous environments, which are unhealthy and unsustainable for both the individual and the system as a whole.

The Industrial era's greatest strength, an uncompromising faith in technology, is also one of its greatest weaknesses. The simplistic adoption of any given technology, without an understanding or systemic feedback mechanisms to track its impact on society, is the ethos of a child, an immature civic morality. To paraphrase the technology thinker Marshall McLuhan, first we shape technology then technology shapes us. We still grasp to understand how technology shapes us, yet, we rapidly transform from industrial technologies to a new era, for lack of a better term, of information technologies.

These new, electronic, information technologies are transforming industrial economies. Technology has been the fundamental shaping force of the modern era. Developing an understanding of the power of this shaping, will enable us to meet some of challenges we face as new technologies now reshape industrial society. It is the understanding of this shaping process, call it design, that will be a fundamental force and positive potential of the next economic era. We are leaving the era of industry and embarking on great new experiments of design. To succeed, we will need the active participation of each of us helping shape our individual and collective lives. We must all be active participants in creating the thinking, tools, institutions, politics, and culture of the design economy.

II.

"The cycle of the machine is now coming to an end. Man has learned much in the hard discipline and the shrewd, unflinching grasp of practical possibilities that the machine has provided in the last three centuries: but we can no more continue to live in the world of the machine than we could live successfully on the barren surface of the moon." - Lewis Mumford

There are many components of the Industrial era that differentiate it from the Agrarian era. Among the most important were the great developments in the sciences of physics and chemistry. The thinking in these two areas led to the great technological advances that were the foundations of industrialization; the mass forging of iron/steel and the harnessing of energy gained from the burning of fossil fuels—coal, oil, and natural gas.

In just 150 years, these industrial forces transformed the United States. In that time, a matter of just five generations, over three-quarters of the population went from working in agriculture to just one percent today. We went from mostly rural living to urban, and mid-way, with the infrastructure of the automobile in place, to extensively suburban. A republic, founded mainly of small farm landowners and merchants at the end of the Agrarian era, was transformed into a population of mostly wage earners. Economic power initially quite diffuse, gradually became ever more concentrated into fewer and fewer mega-corporations—the great institutional inventions of the Industrial era.

Over the entire era, political economy became increasingly centralized. Industrial production, its implementation with the machine and the assembly line enabled mass production and mass consumption, fostering centralization of production and distribution. Local diversity and knowledge was overwhelmed by the homogeneity of industrial technology. The distributed political economy of a small farm agrarian society was transformed into centralized government in Washington DC and centralized control in the industrial mega-corporation. Not only did government power become increasingly centralized, but, with the introduction and eventual domination of broadcast media, the processes of politics did as well. This centralization led to the techniques of mass manipulation of politics and the growth of bureaucracy for mass control in governance.

Over time, the politics, culture, and institutions of the industrial era took on the appearance of the machines and technologies of industry itself, and this machine has become increasingly unsustainable.

III.

"Unfortunately, once an economy is geared to expansion, the means rapidly turn into an end and 'the going becomes the goal.' Even more unfortunately, the industries that are favored by such expansion must, to maintain their output, be devoted to goods that are readily consumable either by their nature, or because they are so shoddily fabricated that they must soon be replaced. By fashion and build-in obsolescence the economies of machine production, instead of producing leisure and durable wealth, are duly canceled out by the mandatory consumption on an even larger scale." —Lewis Mumford

As various industrial philosophies and schools of thought were developed, the most important to emerge was the idea of industrial capital and its unquenchable need for growth. Unlimited production and unlimited consumption facilitated infinite growth, becoming the *raison d'etre* of the entire system. Coupled with the notion of any technology capable of being developed should be utilized, growth and technological innovation became their own necessary ends, dominating any and all others.

The industrial era's great perpetual machine's fundamental product was infinite growth. It created a society divided into two components; production and consumption, in which a person needed a job in the production aspect to gain the benefits of consumption. The system is only considered healthy if it produces more every year. It is only considered beneficial if consumption increases each year. It is a system that values quantitatively, and scarcity is confused with qualitative value.

Just as the end of the Agrarian era did not end agriculture, the end of the Industrial era will see neither the end of industry or its fundamental importance, however it will require increasingly less labor and will rapidly be less defining of the economy, politics, and culture of human society. There are two main reasons for this: 1)The knowledge and the technologies of the sciences of quantum physics and biology are adding to, replacing, and surpassing the impact of earlier technologies developed with the understandings of Newtonian physics and chemistry, 2)The doctrine of unlimited growth, necessitating unlimited production and unlimited consumption is meeting natural resource and ecological systems constraints. Fortunately, the first element can provide solutions for the second.

Knowledge of the planet's material limits, shown in part by growing environmental problems including decreasing biodiversity, collapse of ocean fisheries, and climate change, all instigated by industrial technologies, have in recent years raised important questions on the feasibility of unlimited industrial growth. At the same time, limits are being revealed in supplies of natural resources, particularly oil, the lifeblood of industrial modernity. However, as was recently described in the *Financial Times*, oil is certainly not the only resource limit,

> "The broad story is of depletion. Most of the easily obtainable resource deposits have already been exploited and most usable agricultural land is already in production. Natural resource discoveries, where they continue to occur, tend to be of a lower quality and are more costly to extract. Meanwhile, the dwindling supply of unutilised land faces competing demands from biodiversity, biofuels and food production."

As technology confronts various environmental constraints, the Newtonian physics and chemistry based paradigm is transforming to one of quantum physics and biology. It is the difference between fossil fuel power and solar energy, broadcast media and the Internet, and chemical farming and bio-knowledgeable sustainability, simply, a greater understanding of natural systems. These sciences and their technologies are rapidly changing industrial society, combined with ever growing environmental challenges, they create the need for a new understanding of political economy. It's a sensibility that rejects the idea of infinite growth and the tyranny of unlimited production rewarded by unlimited consumption, while embracing the transition from the industrial economy to the design economy.

IV.

> "Without constant enticement and inveiglement by advertising, production would slow down and level off to normal replace-

ment demand. Otherwise many products could reach a plateau of efficient design which would call for only minimal changes from year to year." —Lewis Mumford

The steam engine, comprised of steel and coal, both best symbolizes the industrial era and represents what might be considered its quintessential tool for shaping and defining the entire era. With the steam engine, the technology of Newtonian physics fundamentally reshaped the natural landscape in less than two centuries to a greater degree than agrarian technologies allowed humanity to reshape the planet in over ten-thousand years.

In this new era of design, the tool which might both symbolize the era and become its greatest shaping instrument is the networked microprocessor. A technology of quantum physics, and while presently fired by fossil fuels, though soon to be powered by renewable energy sources, the networked microprocessor produces and then communicates the fundamental element of the design economy—information.

The term information is used quite informally, though the most general and widest definition might be the most accurate. The bits, numbers, words, sounds, images, and even touch sensations produced by humanity, our technology, and our systems are all information. We gain value from information using design. That is, information not utilized for some aspect of design, whether it is scientific, economic, political, or entertainment becomes noise, though some people's noise might be valued in others design, but without design—editing, communication and utilization—information basically remains noise.

The creation of information and its design have been fundamental aspects of civilization since its inception, in fact one could argue it is civilization. Power in civilization has always coincided with the control of the creation, editing, and communication of information, particularly that information essential to the society's core functioning. For example, the calendar, necessary for proper functioning of agrarian society was controlled by both government and religious ruling classes.

Five hundred years ago, with the dawn of the modern scientific revolution, the printing press was also birthed, revolutionizing the communication of information. In the 20th century, the invention of electronic broadcast media again saw a revolution in information creation and communication, having very dramatic impacts on society—economically, politically and culturally. The control of creation, editing, communication, that is the design of information is a fundamental aspect of political economic power in any society. The invention of the printing press helped loose control of the Catholic church and the established aristocracy across Europe, while the establishment of broadcast media helped Washington D.C. and the Fortune 500 gain control in the United States.

The networked microprocessor, again both as symbol and practical tool, brings a new information revolution to our society, allowing the creation, editing, and communication of information at rates exponentially higher than anytime in previous human history. Importantly, information plays an increasingly fundamental role in production processes and the product itself. Only several decades old, this information revolution has initially been co-opted by the industrial era as a means to "better" industrial processes. However, the true value of this information revolution will not be gained via industrial valuations, just as agrarian values and definitions could not give industry its true value. Increasingly, industrial constraints are hindering our ability to obtain the true value in utilizing information—the value of design—which is not gained simply quantitatively by increasing production and consumption, but qualitatively through design. The greatest value gained from design will be in using fewer resources, less labor, and in many cases less consumption, for these things, industrial society has limited value.

An example of this is the process of automation, removing human labor from the industrial machine, allowing less human labor for the production of the same amount of product. However, in taking the line-worker out of the production process, you are also taking away former and would be future workers from the labor that allows them to consume. While the American economy is much larger than it was 50 years ago, we still produce a similar amount of steel, but due to automation, the American steel industry today uses one-third or less of the labor to produce the same amount of steel. This process is going to continue and eventually, in the not too distant future, remove human labor from most industrial processes. Information is cheaper than labor.

Yet, just as designing fully robotic factories of the future will have a transformational impact on production, it will have an even more important, one could say transcendent, impact on consumption. In many ways, industrial economy's consumption components are primeval. They are based on elemental components of human existence, such as food, shelter, security, and reproduction. These primary elements of existence have deep roots in the human psyche. As the capitalist industrial economy grew, and thus the need for infinite growth, it combined with the 20th century information broadcast revolution to create a mass consumption economy and culture based on the exploitation of primal urges, creating in many senses a neanderthal economy. One only need watch, listen to, or see a few minutes of most advertising to experience its manipulation of hunger, fear, and sex, most of it having little to do with the product.

It is this playing to primal urges that stokes the growth economy and stokes mass cultural anxiety. For primal urges can never be satisfied so much as only satiated, yet our growth economy disallows even this. In fact, it does just opposite, constantly and incessantly stoking primal urges for the ends of ever more consumption and thus endless growth. It is in fact only the rational mind that can soothe primal urges by understanding them and not allowing them to endlessly dictate behavior.

If we were to borrow from the Ancient Greeks, and separate life into thoughtfulness and primal urges, the American economy would resemble a massive Bacchanalian orgy. We would be wise to remember the Greeks looked at these primal urges as essential and enjoyable aspects of existence, but they also walled-off unmitigated enjoyment into a festival. The idea of the primal as a foundation for society, would be foreign to the Greeks, for civilization by its very definition is thoughtfulness, the smoothing of primal urges with rational thought.

Seventy-percent of the American economy is consumer based and to thrive relies on hundreds of billions of dollars of advertising endlessly triggering deep primal urges—it is literally uncivilized. What we need to do is get more thoughtful about our consumption, that is, to better design our economy on available knowledge using information as a tool. Instead of reward exclusively through consumption, reward will be gained by participating in design. This will lead to less gross consumption, which is not only okay, but essential as we reach the limits of natural resources and the destruction of ecological systems. Paradoxically, the primeval ecological elements which birthed the human species, and on which our survival remains completely reliant, need to be saved by the uniquely human concept of civilization.

We live in a time where Newtonian physics and industrial technologies need to be transformed by our 19th and 20th century knowledge of biology. Most revolutionary is the concept of evolution and natural selection. In nature, life changes continuously through constant reproduction and mutation. It is with natural selection—the choosing process of the greater environment—that new designs move forward or are rejected. We must adopt this thinking for our political economy, with an understanding that each of us are components of the greater human environment known as civilization. We are the selection process in creating the future, both individually and just as importantly collectively. As we continue to reshape our civilization and the planet itself using technologies derived from the processes of rational thought, decisions cannot be left to simply exploiting primal urges. We must use the same thought and deliberation to design the economy, politics, and culture of our civilization. That is the design economy.

The greatest example of how design will become paramount is with energy. The Industrial age was built on the seemingly unlimited supply of cheap fossil fuels, combined with failure to assess the negative costs for the environment. What developed, particularly in the United States, was an economy dependent on massive energy waste. This now immoral waste is apparent in all aspects of energy use, for example lighting, heating, and cooling, however it is most easily exemplified with the U.S. automobile culture. It is the height of inefficiency to take a one-hundred-fifty to two-hundred pound person, encase them in a couple tons of steel powered by a highly inefficient internal-combustion engine, and use that as the main means of transportation, restructuring the entire infrastructure, much of the economy, and the culture itself.

The automobile represents the perfect product for the Industrial era. It is labor intensive, that was before increasing automation, resource intensive in metals and other materials, and requires massive amounts of energy. They also need to be relatively frequently replaced, they are certainly not built to last. Every aspect of the automobile added to the Gross National Product, the industrial era's ultimate barometer of economic fair weather, while its impacts on the greater ecological systems from extraction of resource material to its pollution of air and water systems were at first ignored and then socialized.

Now in direct contradiction to industrial economy, a design economy would look to design transportation using the least amount labor, resources, and energy. It would look at the uses of transportation, and then design processes which would be more efficient. For example, the centralizing of goods distribution in warehouse size grocery and department stores, requiring people drive two ton automobiles to pick up five pounds of foodstuffs or two pounds of clothing is crazily inefficient. Much better would be to design neighborhoods where people could walk and bike to pick up their day to day necessities, allowing most of the physical goods distribution to occur using larger more efficient vehicles.

Now the same inefficiencies, off-book environmental degradation, and resource exploitation occur throughout the industrial economy, in fact, distressingly, such things in many ways define a healthy and vibrant industrial economy. We need to redefine much of this value, understanding if we concentrate on design first, production and consumption second, instead of an economy based on ever greater growth, simply more and more stuff, we will have an economy of enough, providing a quality of life much more satisfying and substantial than that gained by quantitative value.

V.

"The ordinary person senses the greatness of the odds against him even without thought or analysis, and he adapts his attitudes unconsciously. A huge passivity has settled on industrial society. For people carried about in mechanical vehicles, earning their living by waiting on machines, listening much of the waking day to canned music, watching packaged movie entertainment and capsulated news, for such people it would require an exceptional degree of awareness and an especial heroism of effort to be anything but supine consumers of processed goods." — Marshall McLuhan, *The Mechanical Bride: Folklore of Industrial Man*

Humanity's great agrarian era produced agrarian government systems, economies, and cultures. Human life and human identity derived overwhelmingly from the processes of farming. The much shorter two-centuries old industrial era redefined life. The processes of production and consumption became the overwhelming dual identities of individuals and our institutions that evolved to foster the processes of unlimited industrial growth. As we move into the design economy, increasingly the most imperative questions will be what are the roles, identities, institutions, and processes of design.

Design has been part of human history before the beginning of civilization. It has at times played an instrumental role with the designing of hunting tools, farming implements, and industrial technologies. However today, information, the raw material of design, is becoming not simply ubiquitous but fundamental to every aspect of human life. For example, with our knowledge of DNA comes the ability to manipulate the very information codes of life itself.

Presently, many of the processes of design—the creation of information, its editing communication, and finally decision making for its utilization—are in turns both centralized and insufficient. We need to evolve our institutions, organizations, and individual roles to understand that design is increasingly the primary value of political economy, ultimately creating a value shift from industrialization's quantitative value of infinite growth based on unlimited production and consumption to design's more qualitative values of participation, efficiency, elegance, and enough.

If we look at the processes of design today, we see rapid change. Companies, governments, NGOs, and individuals each year produce an exponentially greater amount of information. In the distribution and communication of information, paper is in great decline as electronic media explodes. Creation and communication of news and public affairs, once the exclusive domain of print, was supplanted by electronic broadcast media by the mid-20th century, and is now rapidly being replaced by the networked microprocessor, creating both a plethora of real and potentially valuable information, but also an unprecedented amount of noise, with little or no value. Noise grows as what could be useful information is communicated with no ability for the individual or organization to place it in meaningful context.

Yet, even the gaining of valuable information is hamstrung in utilization as the decision making for political economy remains tremendously centralized. Much of the wealth, and thus the economic decision making of the nation is concentrated in the Fortune 500. At the same time, over the past century as government power became more greatly centralized in Washington DC, political decision making became further and further removed from state, localities and the citizen. As previously noted, information both for consumer purposes and electoral decisions—the only direct role citizens have in political decision making—is overwhelmingly manipulative and based on primal motivations, not the rational decision making necessary for civilized design.

In an information environment overwhelmed with noise, the individual is increasingly at a disadvantage as it becomes ever more difficult to filter or more appropriately edit information so that it might be utilized. Individuals face a tsunami of information provided with little or no context, making it difficult to put any of it to use. In contrast, the industrial organization, be it the Fortune 500 or a federal bureaucracy has advantage in contextualizing much of the information they need to make decisions, not to mention the power to then implement. Thus, they can staff tremendous numbers for simply editing information flows. However, over time, this can also become a disadvantage in large organizations and bureaucracies as information channels become locked-in, leading to stagnation and inability of the organization or bureaucracy to utilize new information. And just as importantly, these large structures play a role in protecting the status-quo, manipulating information flows to suit their self-interests.

We need to begin to evolve our institutions, organizations, and bureaucracies with an understanding that the creation, processing, and utilization of information is not simply an essential component, but the predominant one. This means both changing our institutions and creating new ones. It necessitates reviving the idea of associations, an essential part of the American republic's democratic history. As Tocqueville wrote of the vibrant agrarian American republic, "Americans of all ages, all stations in life, and all types of dispositions are forever forming associations." Yet, this necessary distributed formation of associations has been lost or replaced by the centralized order instilled by the Fortune 500 and Washington DC.

A design economy needs to birth millions of design associations. They will be both local and geographically based and distributed electronically across global networks. They will stand alone and be distributively tied. These associations will create, edit, communicate, and utilize information, that is they will design. Most importantly, they will provide the individual, the citizen, the consumer a mean to be an active participant of the design economy.

In the end, the foundation of the design economy is not stuff, it's people. And for the design economy to transcend industrial life, people are going to need to be freed from industrial structures, most essentially the processes of unlimited production and consumption. People are going to need the time, and just importantly society is going to have to value the processes of design. Which means people as both individuals and collectively as associations are going to be valued as creators, editors, communicators and decision makers, in short we must revalue the citizen.

VI.

"It would be curious...if an idea, the fugitive fermentation of an individual brain, could, of natural right, be claimed in exclusive and stable property. If nature has made any one thing less susceptible than all others of exclusive property, it is the action of the thinking power called an idea, which an individual may exclusively possess as long as he keeps it to himself; but the moment it is divulged, it forces itself into the possession of every one, and the receiver cannot dispossess himself of it. Its peculiar character, too, is that no one possesses the less, because every other possesses the whole of it. He who receives an idea from me, receives instruction himself without lessening mine; as he who lights his taper at mine, receives light without darkening me. That ideas should freely spread from one to another over the globe, for the moral and mutual instruction of man, and improvement of his condition, seems to have been peculiarly and benevolently designed by nature, when she made them, like fire, expansible over all space, without lessening their density in any point, and like the air in which we breathe, move and have our physical being, incapable of confinement or exclusive appropriation. Inventions then cannot, in nature, be a subject of property. Society may give an exclusive right to the profits arising from them, as an encouragement to men to pursue ideas which may produce utility, but this may or may not be done, according to the will and convenience of the society, without claim or complaint from anybody." —Thomas Jefferson, Letter to Isaac McPherson, 1813.

The great transformation from the Industrial era to an era of design will be pushed by the increasing knowledge of science and its technologies, but one of the great changes will be revaluing of political economy, from an overemphasis on product to a greater valuing of process. After all, life is not product, it is process, an understanding enabling us to greater value that which makes us human. Using knowledge from quantum physics and biology will allow us to create more organic systems, with people not technology, and design not product as the greatest mediators of value. Integral to the whole process will be information and how it is created, controlled and communicated, and in so doing we will revalue information.

Industrial markets pay little value to information, value is predominately gained on physical goods. While we can and must evolve markets to place more value on information content, in many ways what must be revived and placed prominent is the value modern democratic politics places on the free flow of information. This is part of the American system little valued in economic dogma, yet essential to not only the health of the American political system, but just as much to the vibrancy of the American economy. We need to add the political back to the economy.

In the American constitution, you will find certain foundational pillars on the control of information necessary to build the design economy. The ideas of free speech and freedom of the press remain just as important today as then. But they must be defined anew in an era of networked microprocessors, where each individual's speech can be amplified, every person owns a press, while the Fortune 500 and our own government fight to keep ever more information proprietary.

The constitutional questions of copyrights and patents are essential to this new era. As Jefferson pointed out these are not natural rights but societal creations based on fostering innovation. But again, in industrial America, the benefits of copyrights and patents gained through production become more problematic in an era of design, where information in an organic design political economy becomes something like DNA, necessary to build all the physical processes atop it. Limiting the free transference of this information can cause vast mutations in the entire design political economy.

Today, the Fortune 500 spends millions on lobbying to strengthen patent and copyright law, not to help innovation, but to stifle it and gain further control.

The Internet has given us a few hints on how to evolve design principles. Open distributed networks can create their own order based on an open architecture, that is, allowing all equal access and not discriminating transmission based on content. In the software area, principles such as open source have shown that people can create dynamic stable systems where the information is left open to all to freely manipulate and evolve. These are issues of fundamental importance to the design economy, just as questions about labor and control of the railroads and utilities were to the industrial age.

One of the most interesting changes that might occur is to money itself. Money has an information component, a necessary question for much greater probing is if some of this information can be "socialized", that is, extracted from money and claimed as part of a more robust political culture. An easier way to think about this is how industrial economy in many cases forces information to be turned into product so that it might be valued. However, if we create new associations and evolve our present organizations to understanding the societal value of information, we may gain value from much information without it being monetized. Yet, over years, industrial society and particularly the last few decades has trended in the exact opposite direction, monetizing all aspects of life.

In the end, we must revive and evolve the citizen, our politics, and our government. We need to create value for design, thus valuing the processes of design. Most importantly, we must give value to the citizen, and that means the work of the citizen must be valued. We need to redesign our economy so that production and technology are both second to people.

SELECT BIBLIOGRAPHY

Arnedt, Hannah; *Between Past and Future*

Arnedt, Hannah; *The Human Condition*

Bernanke, Ben; *Essays on the Great Depression*

Boulding, Kenneth; *The Meaning of the Twentieth Century*

Braudel, Fernand; *Memory and the Mediterranean*

Braudel, Fernand; *Civilization and Capitalism*

Cooper, Andrew Scott; *The Oil Kings*

Elliott, J.H., *The Count-Duke of Olivares: The Statesman in an Age of Decline*

Gandhi, Mohandas; *The Story of My Experiments With Truth*

Galbraith, John Kenneth; *Money: Whence it Came, Where it Went*

Goodall, Jane; *Reasons for Hope*

Goodwyn, Lawrence; *Breaking the Barrier*

Goodwyn, Lawrence; *The Populist Moment*

Gould, Stephen Jay, *Times Arrows, Times Cycles*

Greider, William; *Secrets of the Temple*

Hogan, Wesley C.; *Many Minds, One Heart*

Jefferson, Thomas; *Collected Letters*

Keynes, John Maynard; *Treatise on Money*

Keynes, John Maynard; *Economic Possibilities of our Grandchildren*

King Jr., Martin Luther; *Beyond Vietnam: A Time to Break Silence*

McLuhan, Marshall; *Understanding Media*

Mommsen, Theodor; *History Of Rome*

Montesquieu, Charles-Louis de Secondat, *Considerations on the Causes of the Greatness of the Romans and Their Decline*

Mumford, Lewis; *The Myth of the Machine*

Nietzsche, Friedrich; *The Dawn*

Oppenheimer, J. Robert; *Uncommon Sense*

Patal, Raj; *The Value of Nothing*

Phillips, Kevin; *Bad Money*

Polanyi, Karl; *The Great Transformation*

Plutarch, *Lives*

Robins, Nick; *The Corporation That Changed the World*

Smith, Yves; *Econned*

Vidal, Gore; *United States: Essays 1952–1992*

JOSEPH G. COSTELLO

Joe Costello has been at the confluence of politics, communications, economics, and energy for over three decades. Costello worked for over a dozen years running election campaigns from the city council to presidential level, starting with Edward M. Kennedy's presidential campaign in 1980. In 1992, he was Communications Director for California Governor Jerry Brown's presidential campaign where he very successfully helped redefine political communications and campaign fundraising. In 2004, he was a Senior Adviser to Governor Howard Dean's ground breaking presidential campaign.

In the late 1990s, working with a coalition of energy companies and environmental groups, he devised and helped organize a successful statewide campaign to promote solar, wind, and geothermal energy generation to California businesses and local governments. In recent years, he led a marketing campaign for Tree Media's and Leonardo DiCaprio's award winning environmental documentary, The 11th Hour. He has worked with personal computer entrepreneur—Lotus 1,2,3, and Internet pioneer, Mitchell Kapor. He was a

United Nations NGO representative for Mikhail Gorbachev's Global Green USA to the "United Nations Global Summit on Sustainability" in Johannesburg, South Africa 2002, and the "United Nations Convention on Climate Change," in Bali, Indonesia, 2007. He is a graduate of Boston College.

Over the last two decades, Costello became increasingly concerned with the growing corruption and dysfunction of the American political economy. He believes political and economic reform is a necessity and will only be accomplished by the individual political will and collective action of the American people.

Greatest thanks in putting this together to the invaluable help of Jan Frel, and special thanks to Cara Brown and Nadia Conners.

Made in the USA
Charleston, SC
26 May 2012